WALLABY

THE VEGETARIAN WEIGHT LOSS COOKBOOK

Frances Sheridan Goulart

A Wallaby Book
Published by Simon & Schuster
New York

WALLABY and colophon are registered
trademarks of Simon & Schuster

Designed by Irving Perkins Associates

First Wallaby Books Printing April 1982
10 9 8 7 6 5 4 3 2 1
Manufactured in the United States of America
Printed and Bound by Halliday Lithograph

Library of Congress Cataloging in Publication Data

Goulart, Frances Sheridan.
    The vegetarian weight loss cook book.

    "A Wallaby book."
    Includes index.
    1. Reducing diets—Recipes.   2. Vegetarian cooking.
I. Title.
RM222.2.G628   613.2'5   81-18305
                                   AACR2
ISBN 0-671-42826-8

*To my
extraordinary
family,
and to my
extraordinary
secretary, Esme Carroll,
who treats me
like family*

CONTENTS

THE VEGETARIAN WEIGHT LOSS COOKBOOK

I

What's Up, Doc?
An Introduction to Dieting
with Vegetables

SOME HARD FACTS

What's up, doc?

If it's your weight, you have plenty of plump company.

We are living in a land where survival of the fattest seems to be the rule. About one-third of the adult population is overweight by more than 10 percent the normal weight for their height. The National Center for Health Statistics recently released results of a weight study of 13,600 people checked from 1971 to 1974. Women under the age of forty-five weighed 4.7 pounds more, on average, than women of equivalent height checked in a 1960–62 study. Men under the age of forty-five were 3.8 pounds heavier than their counterparts of a decade earlier, and those older than forty-five were 4.8 pounds heavier.

Thus we weigh more, gain more, but need less. Thanks to modern technology, which saves us from expending energy and burning up calories, today's weight-conscious female needs 600 fewer calories (1,800 a day will suffice for most of us rather than 2,400) to stay trim.

What's a body to do?

Diet, of course.

Diets come and go but the end is nowhere in sight. The great American waistline goes on. And on. We spend $10 million a year trying to slim down, though medical experts say there's no reason why we should be a pound heavier at forty-five than we were at twenty-five.

Some of us never have to worry about getting thin again because some of us have never been fat, but if you are at all average and between the ages of twenty and fifty, by now you will have been on 15 major diets lasting an average of two to three months apiece.

Even a little bit of extra weight can be bad for your health. It increases the possibility of disorders such as heart disease, high blood pressure, diabetes, gallstones, varicose veins, back problems, or arthritis either developing or worsening. And, according to the New York Academy of Medicine, maintaining ideal weight is extremely important in the prevention of such diseases, plus many types of cancer, kidney and liver diseases, lung pathology, and even problems in pregnancy and childbirth.

Fat can even be fatal. Former White House nutritionist Jean Mayer, writing in *Preventative Medicine* said, for instance, American men who are only 10 percent overweight have a 20 percent greater risk of dying before their time than men of normal weight.

But you can reduce that risk with a crutch that's only a crunch away.

There are 27,960 diets on record, only 20 of which pass muster. This is not number 27,961. Do-or-die diets are not the way to do away with those extra five to twenty-five pounds you're trying to shed, because a month later you'll be hungry again. But trading up nutritionally by reducing your intake of meat while increasing the amount of fruits, greens, and grains you eat, may be.

The USDA says better nutrition alone could reduce obesity by fifty percent.

In spite of this fact, our annual consumption of fresh foods over the past twenty-five years has inched down 11 percent, while our weight has inched up. It's been forced up, for one reason, says Sydney Abraham, chief of the government's Nutrition Statistics Bureau, by "the continuing problem of overweight linked to the rise of fast food . . . and junk food in the American diet."

But the greening of Americans is also on the rise. At last count, says the Vegetarian Information Society, there were 7 million full-fledged vegetarians in the United States who were meat abstainers for some or even all of the following reasons: A vegetarian diet is better for your health; a vegetarian diet is a lot more economical; it's wrong to kill animals for food; and grain will feed more of the world's population when it's eaten as grain than when it is used to feed livestock.

Another group of us (37.5 million strong) are sometime-abstainers. This group is a high-growth group. No wonder.

Why is it that the string-bean eaters among us remain thinner and more energetic than our burger-eating brethren? According to a recent study of 418 Australian vegetarians reported in the *American Journal of Epidemiology,* besides having lower blood pressure, the group weighed less than meat eaters. And a classic study reported by the *Journal of the American Dietetic Association* that compared vegetarians to others found them to be *twenty pounds leaner* on the average. More recently, a study of young vegetarians conducted by the Harvard School of Public Health found that the men weighed an average of twenty-two pounds below their previous maximum weight. The women in the group had dropped an average of twelve pounds. And this group included lacto-ovo vegetarians (milk-and-egg eaters) and those who simply excluded red meats, as well as vegetarians.

"It is a curious and yet unexplained fact," says one government report, *Nutritional Studies of Vegetarians,* "that vegetarians can eat the same amount of calories as meat eaters, and still gain much less weight. 'Pure' vegetarian men and women average twenty pounds less than the other two groups (meat eaters and milk-and-egg eaters) despite approximately the same caloric intakes and physical activities."

Is it really so curious?

All vegetables, of course, are notoriously low in the "no-no's" that meat is high in: calories, carbohydrates, cholesterol, saturated fat, and appetite-triggering chemicals. Vegetables supply calcium and weight-reducing roughage that meat doesn't, as well as goodly, if nonconcentrated, amounts of some of the harder-to-get amino acids. So when dieting with vegetables you can have your stew (if it's made with parsnips, not pork) and your bread (if it's a prudently portioned slice of potato rye) and eat it, too.

You don't even have to desert desserts while losing weight. Your next cupcake could be no more than a few pureed carrots, squash, or sweet potatoes away . . . when you diet the vegetarian way. And it all lies straight ahead. Read on.

THE VEGETARIAN WEIGHT LOSS DIET: HOW IT WORKS

Dieting the vegetarian way is not a formalized diet; it is a concept based on a wealth of medical and nutritional findings. It is not so much becoming a vegetarian as it is using vegetarian tactics to get thin. The vegetation diet is unlikely to conflict with any formalized diet plan your doctor has approved—low sodium, low fat, reduced sugar, and so on. But before going on *any* diet to lose weight, get a clean bill of health from your physician. And consider the following points.

A vegetarian diet is the oldest, most natural way to lose weight.

Most of the world—80 percent—is vegetarian, and most of the world is thinner than we are.

Non-prime-rib enthusiasts have always been the majority. No wonder. Plant-based eating offers fewer calories, less fat, more fiber, more natural food, more raw food. In fact, the longest-lived peoples of the world—the Hunzas in Pakistan and the Georgians in the Soviet Union—eat a diet consisting mostly of complex carbohydrate foods, with about one-third the fat and one-half the protein of the American diet.

This diet plan is simply man's natural diet, what we evolved on, says Vaughn Bryant, Ph.D., head of the department of anthropology at Texas A. & M. University, who discovered the caveman's diet to be primarily fruits and vegetables (with a few assorted snakes and grasshoppers)—very low in fat, high in carbohydrates and fiber. Bryant, who went on a modified caveman diet by eliminating eggs, butter, oil, and simple sugars, and eating whole-grain pita bread, fruit, potatoes, rice, lean meat, and fish, lost thirty pounds, kept it off, and noted a marked increase in his energy and well-being.

Greens, beans, fruits, and grains are naturally thinning foods. Complex-carbohydrate foods have fewer calories than the high-fat foods. One gram of carbohydrate has 4 calories; one gram of fat has 9 calories. For instance, a large baked potato has 145 calories, while the same size baked potato with one tablespoon of sour cream and butter has 272 calories. A pound of apples has only 263 calories, while a pound of Swiss cheese has 1,610 calories. And so it goes. Complex carbohydrates also lower serum cholesterol and eliminate constipation.

Vegetables fill you up, not out, with their enzyme- and vitamin-rich complex carbohydrates. One of the main benefits of a proper vegetarian diet is its low calorie content relative to the bulk it supplies. For instance, one pound of celery contains only 58 calories; one pound of apples contains 242 calories. But a pound of meat contains about 1,200 calories, and cheese contains about 1,700 calories per pound. Cooked beans contain about 400 calories per pound, and whole wheat bread about 1,000 calories per pound.

A sensible vegetarian diet consisting mainly of fruits and vegetables is low in calories and helps maintain ideal weight.

According to the *American Journal of Clinical Nutrition*, many studies have shown that vegetarians, especially vegans (vegetarians who don't eat dairy products), are thinner than the average non-vegetarian. Studies also found that lacto-ovo vegetarians consume twice to four times as much fiber as nonvegetarians, explaining the predominance of lacto-ovo vegetarians in the low-risk group for such ills as diverticular disease of the colon, appendicitis, cancer of the colon and rectum, hiatus hernia, hemorrhoids, and varicose veins.

Fiber helps spread out the release of food energy and prevents fluctuations in the blood sugar levels that lead to overeating of the wrong foods. In contrast, low-fiber, refined carbohydrates, the kind of chemicals found in both fresh and processed meats, have a profoundly negative impact on blood sugar.

Non-meat-centered diets build health and reduce weight by lowering cholesterol and triglyceride levels.

Nothing will put on fat like fat. Fat contains more calories than any other food component. A good vegetarian diet provides a much lower intake of fat since eggs, whole milk, and high-calorie nuts are eaten sparingly and meat is eaten not at all.

The *American Journal of Medicine* reported that this is thought to account for the lower serum cholesterol levels found in vegetarians. And lower serum cholesterol levels are associated with lower risk of developing cardiovascular diseases. Also, according to the National Cancer Institute, low-fat diets decrease the risk of breast and colon cancer.

Forty percent of the average American's fat intake comes from high-calorie meat—including beef that has been implicated in the development of atherosclerosis and heart disease. Even lean beef is 15 percent saturated fat, and a broiled porterhouse averages 45 percent fat. So, fat chance you'll ever get thin on thick steaks.

According to a study of meat-abstaining Seventh-day Adventists, reported in the *American Journal of Epidemiology*, the group's death rate is only 40 percent as high as that of the porterhouse-loving public. Among pure vegetarians, the death rate is only 25 percent as high. So not only does a low-fat plant-based diet mean fewer pounds, it surely means fewer fat-based ills.

Cancer of the colon and rectum is a major problem in countries whose diet is centered on meat, such as the United States (these cancers kill more than 50,000 men and women in a year). But it is rare in underdeveloped countries where little meat is eaten, as well as in Japan, where the preference is for fish. Cancers of the breast and prostate, too, are more prevalent among meat eaters as stated in *Prevention* magazine.

Again, it is the *fat* that red meats supply in abundance that may be a factor in breast and prostate cancer. Meat eaters have less room in their diet for fiber, and this apparently increases the risk of bowel cancer. What's more, they come in contact with some potent cancer-causing chemicals, like malonaldehyde, which is produced when meat is broken down in the intestines, and nitrosamines, formed from the nitrites used to preserve processed meats.

Meat eaters get a bigger share of other chemicals, too. After years of the widespread use of pesticides, their residues are in everything we eat, in beets as well as beefsteaks. But meat, fish, and poultry give you a really heavy dose of these poisons—thirteen times as much as vegetables, grains, and other plant foods—and a recent study confirms that meat eaters retain more of these harmful chemicals in their bodies.

Plant-based diets consisting of greens, beans, and grains are better balanced and more varied.

"A vegetarian can be well nourished," says the National Academy of Science, "if he or she eats a variety of plant foods and gives attention to critical nutrients."

And vegetarians do.

Not only do plant-based diets offer greater satiety value, they offer greater variety than most meat-inclusive diets. As Frances Moore Lappé points out. "There are only five different kinds of meat and poultry compared with . . . fifty kinds of commonly eaten vegetables; twenty-four kinds of peas, beans, and lentils; twenty fruits; twelve nuts; and nine grains!"

A plant-based weight-loss plan could only be dull if you live by leaf alone.

There are, after all, 800,000 different species of plants on earth. Despite this, farmers concentrate their food-growing and we concentrate our food-eating efforts on a mere 12 species, which form the raw materials for the majority of menus around the world.

Well-planned diets, says the American Dietetic Association, are consistent with good nutrition. But most Americans contemplating a vegetarian diet worry that the absence of meat means the absence of needed protein. But such worries are unfounded, according to Alan M. Immerman, D.C., director of research for the American Natural Hygiene Society and health consultant at the Pawling Health Manor in Hyde Park, New York. He states, "The supposed difficulty with protein on a vegetarian diet is in fact more imagined than real for three reasons: 1) the contribution of green vegetable protein has been ignored, 2) the true protein need is less than commonly assumed, and 3) it is possible to combine two low-value plant proteins and get a protein that is of higher quality than meat protein."

Scientists have found that the actual need for protein is 15 grams per day of 100-value protein, 21.5 grams of 70-value protein, or 30 grams of 50-value protein. 100-value protein means all 8 essential amino acids are in ideal proportions and the body is able to use 100 percent of this protein. If one or more amino acid is not present in the ideal quantity, the value would be expressed as 70- or 80-value protein. A wholesome vegetarian diet easily meets the body's need for protein.

A typical vegetarian diet, say researchers M. G. Hardinge and H. Crooks in the *Journal of the American Dietetic Association,* can actually "exceed twice the minimum requirements for essential amino acids."

An example, says Immerman, is the amount of protein in the following foods: six large leaves of lettuce, 3 grams; one carrot, 1 gram; one cucumber, 1 gram; one tomato, 2 grams; 1 stalk broccoli, 6 grams; half an avocado, 2 grams; one banana, 1 gram; one orange, 1 gram; one pear, 1 gram; a half cup of almonds, 13 grams; a half cup of cooked beans, 7 grams. Total: 38 grams of protein.

Vegetarian-oriented diets prevent obesity by sharply eliminating animal proteins and their dangers.

"Never bolt your door with a boiled carrot," said Benjamin Franklin. But, if it's your refrigerator door, you might give it a try. It's better than a Big Mac.

Eating more vegetables increases your potential for losing weight by improving your health and resistance to disease and eliminating toxins that trigger the appetite, as stated in *Bestways* magazine.

As mentioned before, a vegetarian diet helps you avoid the harmful chemicals found in meat. In 1979, the General Accounting Office of the U.S. government reported that 14 percent of meat in supermarkets contained illegal and potentially harmful residues of animal drugs, pesticides and environmental contaminants. Of 143 chemicals likely to leave residues, "42 are known to cause or are suspected of causing cancer, 20 of causing birth defects, and 6 of causing mutations."

Take animal antibiotics, for instance. About two-thirds of the cattle and nearly all poultry, hogs, and veal calves in the United States are raised on feed laced with drugs, including DES, which is known to cause cancer in humans. These animals consume almost 8 million pounds of antibiotics a year, nearly 40 percent of U.S. production.

Opponents to the feed practice argue that these drug-resistant bacteria could be transferred to meat and poultry products and wind up in the human gastrointestinal tract.

Studies reported by *East-West Journal* show that workers on farms and in slaughterhouses who are in contact with drug-contaminated animal feed or raw meat have a higher percentage of drug-resistant bacteria in their intestines than workers in other occupations.

Monensin, an antibiotic made by soil bacteria, is routinely added to beef and poultry feed to speed weight gain and prevent some kinds of infection. Scientists at the University of Miami School of Medicine suspect that it may contribute to the risk of high blood pressure in normal persons and be particularly dangerous to the hundreds of thousands with coronary artery disease. The scientists also report that residues of monensin remain even in chickens who have been fed the additive for only a week, ending five days before they had been slaughtered. In studying various chicken samples, they detected levels high enough to be potentially injurious to people who regularly have chicken in their diet.

There is also more salmonella than ever. A 1978 USDA study showed thirty-seven percent of six hundred samples of supermarket chickens from eleven states were contaminated—an increase of almost 10 percent over the previous year.

And the contents of an average grocery cart of a Cincinnati family were packed in dry ice and shipped to the University of California for scientific analysis, reported a CBS-TV special in October 1979. Tests were done to detect trace amounts of cancer-causing agents in the frankfurters, hamburgers, milk, butter, and cheese. Dan Rather, the reporter-narrator, noted that "everything that came from livestock showed traces of DDT or dieldrin."

Even cooking meat that seems safe introduces trouble. According to the Carcinogen Information Program at the Center for the Biology of Natural Systems, "The heat of cooking causes a chemical reaction to take place, resulting in the formation of mutagens. Cooking methods which cause the surface of the hamburger to exceed 300° Fahrenheit will produce mutagen-containing hamburgers in less than ten minutes, while similar cooking times at lower temperatures will not."

A ham sandwich a day may have other repercussions.

Nitrites are largely a problem confronting meat eaters, and of course, occur most often in meat such as bacon, ham, and luncheon meats since they are added in the processing. Nitrites also destroy vitamin A, handicap the storage of vitamin A, and depress thyroid function. Sodium nitrite is absorbed and eliminated slowly, so its ill effects may be persistent.

But vegetables—the more the merrier—can help. According to Dr. Tsuneo Kada, a mutation specialist at the National Institute of Genetics in Japan, certain varieties of vegetables can counteract nitrosamines. After extensive experimentation, he found that cabbage, cauliflower, lettuce, radishes, turnips, asparagus, bean sprouts, pumpkin, and peas have the ability to inactivate cancer-causing substances in the stomach. (Onions and most of the fruit he tested did not have this effect.) Dr. Kada speculates that an unidentified enzyme present in certain vegetables is responsible for the cancer-inhibiting effect. This appears to be yet another reason why people eating vegetarian diets have a lower cancer rate than meat eaters.

In fact, every time you have it your way with a Big Mac, you miss out on all the secret ingredients in a bowl of crisp "crucifer vegetables." Crucifer vegetables contain compounds known as indoles, some of which induce a chemical process that can detoxify potential carcinogens. "Scientists suspect that the crucifers work through the indoles. In the process of metabolism, the crucifers will change a carcinogen or potential carcinogen into a nontoxic form," reported the *American Journal of Epidemiology*.

Vegetarian dieting allows you more no-no-s—including potatoes, beans, and rice—than traditional diets.

You needn't steer clear of the traditional no-no's when you're on a no-meat diet. It may surprise you to learn that beans are a great food for weight watchers. One hundred grams, or about 3.5 ounces (a half cup) of cooked rice or red beans is only 118 calories (sprouted beans have only 65 calories per cupful), while the same 3.5 ounces of broiled porterhouse steak yields a whopping 465 calories. And beans have superior fill-you-up value, and are zero in saturated fat.

Not only that, they are superior sources of energizing nutrients. One serving of navy beans has more than five times the pick-me-up potassium of chicken.

Small potatoes are not small potatoes either. They are full-value vitamin-rich foods that help improve the functioning of your appestat. And the underlying cause of overeating, say many researchers, is a disordered appestat, the mechanism that controls your desire for food. Nutritional deficiencies are caused by denatured foods, bad diets, lack of exercise. The body needs sixty different nutrients every day to reward you with optimum health. The only diet that gives you what you need is low in animal fats, and high in natural non-appetite-triggering carbohydrates such as vegetables, grains, and fruits.

Are beans fattening? No, they don't have to be. They may, in fact, offer you preventions and cures.

"Eating a half pound of beans a week might be a good idea that will double your intake of legumes and keep total calories in line," says Ancel Keys, Ph.D., professor emeritus at the Laboratory of Physiological Hygiene at the University of Minnesota.

Why bother?

"If you happen to be interested in cholesterol control, beans or any leguminous seeds merit a prominent place in your diet," say studies in *The British Medical Journal* that link beans to the prevention of other killer diseases. One study suggests that beans may play a beneficial role in the diets of diabetics, and beans as a class produce the lowest rise in blood glucose of all carbohydrate-rich foods tested.

A cup of cooked navy or pea beans contains only 224 calories (about the same number of calories as two big apples). Beans are 20 percent protein and 65 percent carbohydrate with little fat (1.1 grams in a cup of cooked navy beans), and no cholesterol. They are a good source of the B vitamins riboflavin, niacin, and B_6, and supply important minerals like calcium and iron. A serving of beans furnishes half the daily recommended dietary allowance (RDA) of iron for men and about a third of the allowance for women. Beans are rich in potassium and low in sodium. They contribute to the health of our digestive systems and the prevention of such "diseases of Western civilization" as cancer of the colon and rectum, and gallbladder disease.

You can even have your carrot cake and eat it—along with your turnip corn pone, zucchini Danish, and avocado ice cream—lowering your weight and your blood cholesterol a bit with every bite. Just skip the sugar and margarine, and use minimal amounts of butter.

Fruits and vegetables enable you to reduce overall caloric count by as much as 50 percent, especially when coupled with bran and other whole grains, which are superior sources of blood-fat–fighting roughage and pectin (a substance found in fruits and vegetables), rather than with high-calorie sweeteners such as sugar, honey, and other syrups. In this way you can tame a sweet tooth rather than pacify it.

Vegetarian foods increase energy, slow down the aging process, and reduce back sliding.

Ninety-five percent of those who lose weight gain it back. Why? Because most diets do not boost health or maintain your energy level while lowering your weight.

In sharp contrast, says the American Academy of Pediatrics' committee on nutrition, "Those who practice vegetarianism have excellent health. As for weight loss? A vegetarian diet is filling (low-calorie vegetables); low in fat (no meat); high in cleansing fiber and natural carbohydrates for instant energy."

Besides the extra pounds that a poor diet (and that means a vegetable-poor diet) always produces there is fatigue, and even accelerated aging.

"A wrong diet," warns Dr. Hans Kugler in his book *Slowing Down the Aging Process,* "can make you age 10 to 15 times faster. That means if you diet wrong for one week you can do as much damage to your system as 30 weeks of normal aging would do. We interfere . . . with hundreds of chemical reactions . . . we do serious damage to our systems; and that's exactly what happens when you go on one of those diets that limit you to one type of food only."

What seems even worse, perhaps, is that the fatter you are, the fatter you get. "Fat people secrete greater amounts of insulin, leading to hunger pains, overeating, and more fat storage," says Dr. Judith Rodin, a Yale University obesity researcher.

Aside from eliminating calories, medical studies have shown that eating quantities of vegetables can reduce or eliminate many of the infirmities associated with aging. For example, researchers have found that the body builds bone up to the age of forty, after which bones begin to deteriorate. Yet, a study of elderly female vegetarians at Michigan State University showed they lost less bone to osteoporosis than a group of the same age that ate meat. Moreover, a diet high in vegetables will provide greater amounts of fiber, offering protection against intestinal diseases so often associated with aging—diseases like diverticulosis, colitis, and plain old constipation.

According to the Longevity Research Institute in California, a diet relying heavily on vegetables, but eliminating fats, sugar, dairy products, caffeine, alcohol, and tobacco, can restore health and vigor even to people with bad hearts when coupled with daily exercise.

Born again body?

The U.S. Senate Select Committee's dietary goals suggest the best way "to ease the problem of weight control" is to eat more natural carbohydrates. "The higher water content and bulk of fruits and vegetables and the bulk of whole grain can bring a longer lasting satisfaction of appetite more quickly than do foods high in fats and refined processed sugars."

A diet high in raw vegetable foods even allows you to cut your intake of high-calorie protein foods by 50 percent.

Is there Karma in a raw carrot? Not only Karma, but 10 percent fewer calories, more protein, potassium, and calcium than in a cooked carrot, plus 13 milligrams of ascorbic acid. It's the same story with bananas, broccoli, spinach, soybeans, and more, if you are shooting for low weight and high health.

Switzerland's Bircher-Benner Clinic and Boston's Hippocrates Health Institute recommend a diet of 60 percent raw food and fresh juices to prevent or reverse degenerative diseases such as arthritis or diabetes.

One sports physiologist had a group of male athletes gradually change over to a purely raw-foods diet from their usual regimen of high-fat and high-protein foods. The diet was strictly supervised, and the men's metabolism and athletic achievements were also monitored. Researchers found that there was no lessening of athletic prowess.* Indeed, the athletes' performances actually improved during the raw-foods period.

Why do unfired foods light your fire and lower your weight?

When certain meats or fish are cooked, less protein is available to the body because high temperatures actually change the biochemical structure of the protein elements and make them only partly digestible. But studies at the Max Planck Institute of Nutritional Research show that if you eat protein foods raw instead of cooked, you need only half the usual amount of protein.

Need another reason raw is beautiful? Certain fungicides which are widely used on today's produce form dangerous chemicals when they are heated, says Dr. William H. Newsome of Canada's Department of Health and Welfare Food Research Division and Bureau of Chemical Safety. Cooked tomatoes, for example, were found to contain ten to ninety times more ETU (a fetus-deforming and cancer-causing compound) than raw tomatoes from the same garden. Dr. Newsome's studies reveal that ETU is the heat-caused end product of the widely used EBDC fungicides. "The amount of ETU which forms during cooking depends on the amount of fungicide residue on the vegetable skin," Dr. Newsome

* Charles Gerras, ed., *Feasting on Raw Foods* (Emmaus, Pa.: Rodale Press, 1980).

explains. "But generally, the amount of ETU in cooked vegetables was about fifty times more than in uncooked vegetables."

A few simple rules to follow to keep a balanced, protein-rich vegetarian menu are:

> 1. Complementary protein mixtures combine two plant protein foods that have opposite amino acid strengths and weaknesses. An excess in one food compensates for a deficiency in the other, and the combination of the two creates a complete, more usable protein. For example: Beans and wheat are fine foods alone but twice as good for you if you eat them together in the same dish or at the same meal.
>
> 2. Complement grains with dried beans and wheat germ; complement dried beans with grains, nuts, seeds, and wheat germ; complement nuts and seeds with dried beans and wheat germ.
>
> 3. Grains, dried beans, nuts, and seeds are more beneficial served with eggs and dairy products.

If your weight is a long way from ideal, or even a short way, the next question is: How do you figure out how many calories you *do* need?

Simple.

> 1. Simply multiply your ideal weight by 15. If you are very active, multiply your ideal weight by 18. For instance, if your ideal weight is 120, multiply by 15 to get 1,800 calories a day.
>
> 2. Every pound on your body is worth 3,500 calories. So, to lose a pound, you have to cut back 3,500 calories—a loss you can spread out over a week or a month. The longer you take, the better, in terms of nutrition. To lose a pound a week, for example, subtract 500 calories from the amount you have been eating each day. You can use your ideal weight in an alternate method of estimating your total calories. Simply multiply your ideal weight by 12.
>
> 3. If you want to lose a pound a week to reach 120, subtract 500 calories from 1,440. Eat 940 calories a day until you get down to your goal. But *only cut back that extensively if you are under a doctor's supervision.* And remember, such a low-caloric intake should not be sustained longer than six weeks without medical supervision.

For example, how to get what's coming to you for lunch. Have a tofu-avocado sandwich made with 100 percent whole grain bread and generously slathered with alfalfa sprouts and washed down with a glass of skim or low-fat milk, plus a nice, fresh, raw apple. You have dipped into all four food groups and the nutritional impact of this lunch has been potent. You've had plenty of protein, not too much fat, lots of fiber, and a generous lacing of vitamins and minerals.

BEFORE YOU EAT AND DIET . . .

What about calories and nutrients you need each day? After all, if you're a virile man you can't get by on 1200 meat-free calories, can you? No.

Having determined your level of health, then taking into consideration your age, build, and present weight, here's about what you should weigh to hang in there and stay healthy:

RECOMMENDED WEIGHT IN RELATION TO HEIGHT *

| Height | MEN | | WOMEN | |
	Average	Range	Average	Range
4 ft 10 in			102	92–119
4 ft 11 in			104	94–122
5 ft 0 in			107	96–125
5 ft 1 in			110	99–128
5 ft 2 in	123	112–141	113	102–131
5 ft 3 in	127	115–144	116	105–134
5 ft 4 in	130	118–148	120	108–138
5 ft 5 in	133	121–152	123	111–142
5 ft 6 in	136	124–156	128	114–146
5 ft 7 in	140	128–161	132	118–150
5 ft 8 in	145	132–166	136	122–154
5 ft 9 in	149	136–170	140	126–158
5 ft 10 in	153	140–174	144	130–163
5 ft 11 in	158	144–179	148	134–168
6 ft 0 in	162	148–184	512	138–173
6 ft 1 in	166	152–189		
6 ft 2 in	171	156–194		
6 ft 3 in	176	160–199		
6 ft 4 in	181	164–204		

* Height without shoes, weight without clothes. Adapted from the Table of the Metropolitan Life Insurance Co.

And you can do all this and lose weight as long as you go lightly on the bread (use thin slices and opt for open face), heavy on the sprouts, slice the tofu and avocado in moderate portions, and skip the butter and mayo.

And how about food groups? You can't just get all your calories in sprouted lentils or tofu, can you? No, again.

The body needs some forty different nutrients a day and this is a need that cannot be met without a variety of foods.

1. *Protein*

You may not need the meat but you do need the nutrients meat supplies—especially protein. As a dietary vegetarian, even a transitory or temporary one, men need roughly 57 grams a day, 47 if you are female.
Sources: Vegetables, dried beans and peas, soy products, nuts, seeds.

2. *Carbohydrates*

If a vegetarian diet shines in any one area, it is here. Carbohydrates supply energy and fiber, and work together with protein and fats to keep the whole body well and capable of repairing itself when breakdowns occur.

What's more, without sufficient carbohydrates, you may wind up with not only less energy but brain-fade. According to the *New York Times Magazine*, September 20, 1981, the higher the carbohydrate-to-protein ratio—with calories kept constant—the livelier the animal. In addition, those on a diet with a high carbohydrate-to-protein ratio eat less and lose weight whereas those on a high-protein, low-carbohydrate diet eat more and also gain weight.

Remember, too, the carbohydrates that vegetables and grains also provide are a valuable source of fiber as well as of vitamins and minerals. Your daily need is for 100 grams or slightly more carbohydrate.
Best sources: Fruits, corn, cereals, breads, potatoes, noodles.

3. *Fats*

These should comprise 10 to 30 percent of your daily diet caloric intake.

Best sources: Oils (avoid hydrogenated), peanuts, walnuts, avocados.

4. Essential Vitamins and Minerals

A balanced diet is important when you are cutting calories, preferably supplemented by at least one multi-vitamin daily for anyone under even mild stress. It is important to include foods from each group. This is even more essential when you are reducing. You are probably dropping desirable as well as undesirable elements from your eating routine.

Best sources:
A (retinol): carrots, green vegetables—800–1,000 micrograms
B_1 (thiamine): whole grains, legumes, nuts, green vegetables—101.5 milligrams
B_2 (riboflavin): green vegetables—1.2–1.7 milligrams
B_3 (niacin): peanuts, whole grains, legumes—12–20 milligrams
B_6 (pyridoxine): potatoes and other vegetables, whole grains—2 milligrams
C (ascorbic acid): citrus fruits, cabbage, melons, strawberries, tomatoes, fresh potatoes, green leafy vegetables—40–60 milligrams
Vitamin D: egg yolk, fortified and evaporated milk, exposure to sunlight—10 micrograms.
Vitamin E: Salad oils, shortening, margarine—8–10 milligrams
Zinc: wheat germ, yeast, legumes—15 milligrams
Iodine: Iodized salt, foods grown in coastal areas, seaweeds—150 micrograms.

5. Even more important than food groups are the foods themselves. "Good" foods that are moderate in calories, that contribute amounts from more than one of these groups include: Sprouts, brown rice, dark green vegetables, wheat germ (in moderation), tofu, yogurt (low fat), eggs, buttermilk, cottage cheese, most fresh fruits and vegetables.

A bologna (meat group) sandwich made with white bread (grain group), served with potato chips (vegetable group), and topped off with a chocolate milkshake (dairy group), may satisfy your basic four-food-group needs in theory, but, in fact, it has done little more than supply you with the raw materials out of which deficiencies are born.

Also, in point of fact, a thoughtful diet that includes dairy foods as well as meat usually leads to excess protein intake. It is exceedingly low in vitamins and minerals and sadly lacking in fiber. This kind of high-salt, high-fat, high-sugar meal sets you up as a prime target for obesity, cavities, diabetes, high blood pressure, constipation, stroke, and chronic fatigue.

II

Carrot Tops: Profiles of America's Top Ten Diet Vegetables

THE CARROT

Chief among the dieter's "food friends" are carrots, one of the most beloved among vegetables with visible vitamins (that characteristic color indicates an abundance of the substance called carotene, otherwise known as pro-vitamin A). There are 6,000 units of vitamin A in one five-and-one-half-inch carrot (only liver has more), B_1 and B_2, lots of natural sodium, plenty of pure phosphorus—free organic calcium, some protein, iodine, and enzymes in the raw juice, and if you eat or use the tops, you get iron and vitamin C as well as E. And equally important to inflation fighters—twenty carrot sticks yield only 20 crunchy calories. And while fruits and leafy greens are only a so-so source of fiber, root vegetables like carrots have twice as much fiber.

Doctors used carrots long before cooks did. Healers say they are a powerful cleansing food. A large amount of carrot carbohydrate is one of the most effective means of changing the intestinal flora from a putrefactive to a nonputrefactive type.

Carrot juice has been used as a cure-all in cases of bronchitis and various stomach ailments. It even fights wrinkles, say some folk medics. Today, carrots are grown in half the home gardens of America and are prized especially for the vitamin A they provide free of the saturated fat that's usually found in other vitamin-A rich foods, such as egg yolks, liver, and butter. Carrots also have a wide variety of uses in cooking, making naturally sweet soups and juices and good sauce extenders. You can even make a chemical-free Easter egg dye from the leaves or juice, a "hamburger helper" from the raw pulp, and a sugar. Carrots can even be percolated for a tasty coffee substitute. Herbs especially compatible with carrots in cooking include allspice, ginger, caraway, mint, and nutmeg.

Carrots belong to the same family as celery, parsnips, caraway, and dill. The Greeks called the carrot *karoton*. The English word carrot comes from the French *carrotte*, which derives from the Latin *carota*, coming from an entirely different Greek word—a verb meaning "to burn," probably due to the vegetable's color.

Carrots grow in all shapes, sizes, and colors. There are Asian types with bulbous purplish red roots, and pale and deep yellow, red, and even white types. Carrot roots may be spherical or cylindrical, and at least one Asian variety grows a yard long. The most popular carrot in the United States is the Mediterranean variety. The best varieties of it have no fibrous central core. Carrots were cultivated in the Mediterranean area before the Christian era but did not become popular as a food until about the thirteenth century A.D. in Europe. But by the sixteenth century they were being grown all over Europe, arriving in America before the Pilgrims. This was one crop the Indians adopted rather than introduced and it soon became a favorite. Cultivated carrots descended from wild carrots, which still grow abundantly. This wild ancestor is actually an herb with a small, tough taproot that was once slightly poisonous but through cultivation became edible.

Today, carrots are among our cheaper, easier to come by, easy to grow vegetables. One way to store carrots for more immediate use is to chop, scrub and store them in a jar full of water. Mature carrots should be used up within two weeks.

Carrots can be stored for months at the right cool temperature. Healthy looking leafy crowns is the sign that the roots will be tender and crunchy.

THE TOMATO

What's green and red and bred all over? Tomatoes, the number three favorite in America's vegetable sweepstakes. Ninety-five percent of all America's gardens grow this juicy member of the nightshade family.

And why not? A tomato is no lemon nutritionally. One average size *pomodoro* has as much ascorbic acid as a half grapefruit, 1,785 I.U. (international units) of vitamin A (one-third the daily allowance), along with potassium, phosphorus, magnesium, and calcium, and only 35 calories.

Tomatoes, which originated in Mexico, were grown only as ornamental plants until the mid-1800s.

Today, there are five hundred varieties grown, with cherry and beefsteak leading in popularity. So-called hard-slicing types found out of season are actually green tomatoes that have been gassed with ethylene to produce redness. While the Italian plum is the best type for sauces, the yellow pear tomato can be turned into an instant jam by simply chopping and simmering thirty minutes with a little sweetening.

Buy them red, firm, and above all, ripe. The tomato's unique balance of sweet and sour sensuality depends on ripeness. A tomato that's too green will taste flat and sour. If overripe, it tastes bland.

What if your tomato isn't ready when you are? Put it in a plastic bag with a banana or an apple. The fruits produce a natural gas called ethylene which will ripen the tomatoes in a day or two.

Gardener's tip: Raising your own tomatoes? Sprinkle a cup of baking soda or Epsom salt around the base of each plant a month after planting to increase both sweetness and productivity.

THE EGGPLANT

Eggplant is a member in good standing of the potato family, the nightshade family, and is actually a fruit—a member of the berry family—that is eaten like a vegetable. It probably originated in India in prehistory. It is sometimes known as *aubergine* (French), while in other places, it's called Guinea squash and Jew's apple.

The Arabs may have been the first people to eat it. But by the sixteenth century, the Spaniards, who believed eggplants to be aphrodisiacal, called them *berenjenas* (apples of love), and northern Europeans of the same period dubbed them "mad apples," convinced that they could cause insanity. They were cultivated as early as 1658 in Brazil.

Eggplants are now popular everywhere. In Japan they are the third most important vegetable. Large purple eggplants are most common here, but white and striped ones are also grown. They grow in all shapes (round, oblong) and sizes. Miniature ones can be cooked whole. Eggplant is even used by some Japanese as a teeth whitener.

Therapeutically, the eggplant has been used for anemia, constipation, to promote the flow of urine, to aid the function of the liver and pancreas, and to lower cholesterol. Used as ornamentals and for vegetable dyes, eggplants are one of the few vegetables that thrive here as well as in the tropics. Foodwise, it can be curried, stir-fried, rolled, steamed, and broiled.

If you are making a nutritional low-calorie U-turn, don't forget to include the passionate, purple eggplant. Here's what three-and-a-half ounces give you: calories, 19; protein, 1.0 grams; fat, .2 (very low fat); carbohydrates, 4.1; calcium, 11 milligrams; phosphorus, 21 milligrams; potassium, 150 milligrams, vitamin A, 10 units; vitamin C, 3 milligrams.

To buy this vegetable, select firm, smooth, heavy purplish-black produce with no soft spots or flabby skin. The stem should be green. If you store an eggplant in a plastic bag, it should keep four to five days. One pound yields three cups of diced eggplant.

To prepare: Wash, cut off stem. Peel (if desired). Slice or cube and sauté, fry or use in combination dishes. Or hollow out, stuff, and bake.

Eggplant makes delicious sandwiches. Cut in ⅓-inch slices, then in half. Peel skin, coat with flour seasoned with salt and pepper, and sauté in butter or margarine until golden brown and tender. Serve at once between soft sliced bread.

THE GREEN PEPPER

There is nothing more red, white, and blue than the green pepper—even when it is red all over.

Columbus may have been searching for that precious commodity, black pepper, when he discovered the New World, but what he finally picked and packed to take home was a peck of those colorful capsular fruits which no real cook or gardener among us could live without.

Indeed, America is home, sweet home to the whole sweet clan of capsicums we know, love, and eat year round as bell peppers. Counting the nonbell varieties, it is estimated that the *Capsicum* family may have as many as three hundred members. (Mexico has one hundred and forty varieties of its own.)

In the United States today, there are 53 million acres devoted just to the production of green peppers. According to the USDA, 61 percent of home gardens grow them. And why not? Capsicums contain ten times as much ascorbic acid as most other popular vegetables.

The red pepper is simply a green pepper with bells on in terms of its nutrition and maturation. Despite its hot color, it is the sweetest and mildest since it has been allowed to mellow fully on the vine. This is not to be confused with that other round red pepper, the pimento, which is the sweetest, reddest, and fleshiest of them all.

All this in addition to generous amounts of vitamin A.

Of all the edible gifts from the New World to the old, few have been more valuable or various than genus *Capsicum annum*. Within the century following Columbus's first voyage to the West Indies, American peppers—which are both a spice and vegetable—took root in tropical Asia, Africa, and temperate regions of Europe, probably altering forever the character of national cuisines. The tiny red, yellow, and green chilies made the most fiery impact, but all the capsicums, sweet, hot, or pungent, found acceptance in some corner of the globe. There are almost as many variations in shape, size, color, and "heat" as in varieties.

Having too many peppers is nothing to be in a pickle about. If you are several pecks * to the good, after pickling, have no fear. The uses for sweet green or red bell peppers never seem to peter out. Peppers can be pickled, preserved, spiced, sauced, soured, braised, stewed, ragouted, slivered, frittered, fried, pureed, dried, frozen, and further processed into a seemingly endless procession of main dishes, side dishes, pastas, and breads, and, of course, homemade paprika.

Once you've picked your peck, production of almost anything sweet, sour, or neutral goes.

Need a hassle-free way to peel that tissuey protective skin for easier eating? Broil peppers two inches from the heat for fifteen minutes, turning often till peppers are blistered on all sides. Place them in a plastic bag ten minutes or till cool enough to handle; peel.

The green or bell pepper is one of the most commonly grown of all the garden vegetables. Sometimes it is red, and this signifies a fully ripened pepper, as every home gardener knows. The most readily found variety (out of the hundreds of types and varieties that are grown or can be raised) is the California Wonder.

Peppers are at their peak in August and September, but they are available commercially all year long. Most store-bought peppers come from Texas, California, Florida, or Louisiana.

Besides being extremely low in calories, peppers pack a real nutritional wallop. Green pepper juice has an abundance of silicon, a trace mineral that greatly benefits the nails and hair. Herbalists often recommend the juice of half a green pepper coupled with carrot juice as an aid in cleaning up skin eruptions. Half a raw pepper provides a full day's quota of vitamin C and a red bell supplies even more C, plus additional amounts of vitamin A. They are low in carbohydrates, rich in many essential vitamins and minerals, including calcium, phosphorus, iron, sodium, and magnesium.

Peppers should be stored in a cellophane bag or in damp cloths in the refrigerator. They may be dried for indefinite use.

* Ever wonder how many pickled peppers are in a peck? Reliable delicatessen sources report the figure is 13 to 15 filleted sweet peppers in a quart or about 104 to 120 per peck. Whole hot peppers are packed 18 to 20 to the quart, giving 144 to 160 hot pickled peppers per peck.

LETTUCE AND GREENS

Lettuce is America's favorite green vegetable—and with good reason. All lettuce—from Chinese cabbage to plain old iceberg—is the real secret of a nutritionally rich life. Americans eat $7 billion worth of lettuce each year, approximately 25 percent of our total fresh vegetable consumption. But the one we eat the most is iceberg.

Crisp-headed lettuce, something like the ubiquitous iceberg head lettuce we know today, can be traced back to ancient Babylonian times. An ancestor of our modern varieties, which is the most popular of the four major types available today, was gathered regularly and relished by natives of Asia Minor, according to historians. Head lettuce was a commonly prepared item on supper tables in the sixteenth century in Europe, too. And on this continent, it was one of the first vegetables planted in every colony.

Eighty percent of the iceberg available today comes from either Arizona or California. Why is it called iceberg? Because prior to modern refrigerated produce trucks, it had to be packed for traveling in ice-layered crates. The two types of iceberg found most often are the Imperial type (large, thin, cabbagelike crumpled leaves) and the Great Lakes type (thick, dark-green leaves with a tough texture).

Nutritionally, iceberg is the lesser of the lettuces but the greener it is, the better a source of vitamins A, B, C, and E it is, as well as a source of natural iron, phosphorus, potassium, and calcium.

If you're trading up in the lettuce department, look what a lift you get: A little lettuce like endive contains twice as much iron as clams and oysters, and more than ten times the potassium in a potato. And like all lettuces, it is full of make-you-feel-good fiber.

An even better choice is the wild greens.

The dandelion is one of those rare birds among weeds-cum-greens—every part of it is edible. In fact, though less frequently consumed, even the budhead is rumored to taste like that delectable morsel, the morel, when you fritter and fry it.

The *dent de lion* (lion's tooth) is actually a member of the sunflower or aster family and has been known by a number of names throughout the ages: blow balls, puff balls, heart-fever grass, cankerwort, wild endive, white endive, swine snout, priest's crown, and fairy clock (during its seeding stage).

Dandelions flourish in all cool and temperate zones of the world, almost every month of the year. The roasted roots are a popular coffee substitute, and in France, they are eaten sliced or grated and raw in salads, in much the same way as celery (roots should be dug in the fall while the plant is in full bloom).

But the part that holds the greatest interest for the salad chef is the tangy "greens," which are used both raw and cooked. They must be picked young in the spring (large leaves are better), but can also be harvested again in the fall. This famous weed has six times the vitamin A of ordinary lettuce, and twice the mineral and fiber content. (It is an especially good source of iron and calcium.)

THE POTATO

If you are at all average you eat one hundred and forty potatoes a year. For the vegetarian dieter, potatoes represent the Great White Hope, because potatoes are high in the right kind of starch, rich in fiber so they're filling and not fattening, and 99.9 percent fat free. A medium-size boiled potato has only 90 calories (an equivalent amount of french fries has 400). Ounce for ounce, that's about the same number of calories as an apple, fewer calories than a cup of yogurt, a three-ounce hamburger patty, or a half-cup of cottage cheese. But eat 'em fresh.

Potatoes have three times more fiber than canned spuds, and 50 percent more than frozen mashed potatoes. They are even richer in potassium (550 milligrams) than bananas and there are 30 milligrams of vitamin C in an average Idaho.

Here's a spud nut's guide to buying and storing:

• Potatoes certified by federal or federal-state inspection as U.S. No. 1 quality are firm, well-shaped, smooth.
• U.S. Extra No. 1 potatoes have fewer defects, are cleaner and more uniform.
• Greening may affect only the skin of potatoes or it may penetrate the flesh. The green portions contain the alkaloid solanine, which causes a bitter flavor. Don't buy them.

 • Never wash potatoes before you store them. Dampness increases the likelihood of decay.

 • The most desirable keeping temperature is 45° to 50° F. Potatoes stored at 70° or 80° F. should be used within a week.

 • General purpose and baking potatoes will keep several months. "New" potatoes should keep several weeks.

THE MUSHROOM

To know one is to love one. Mushrooms are a first-rate fungus among us. And they are gaining in popularity.

Ten years ago, Americans ate an average of about one pound of cultivated mushrooms per year. Last year that amount jumped to 2.1 pounds, according to the American Mushroom Institute. An estimated 380 million pounds of domestic mushrooms and 80 million pounds of imported mushrooms will have been consumed in one year's time.

There are only 90 calories in a whole pound of raw mushrooms (that's 28 calories per three-and-a-half ounces). Mushrooms contain both vitamin D and the B vitamin niacin, plus protein and trace minerals like calcium, iron, and potassium.

For more than thirty centuries, mushrooms have been a gastronomical delight, a botanical mystery. Legend has it that Pluto, Greek god of the lower world in classical mythology, cultivated and enjoyed mushrooms. The pharaohs of Egypt declared mushrooms fit for royalty, and this "mysterious night-growing vegetable" even appeared in Egyptian hieroglyphics. Theophrastus, the Greek historian (371–287 B.C.) wrote about Greeks feasting on mushrooms, and the Roman poet Juvenal (60–140 A.D.) wrote of a Roman epicure who exclaimed, "Keep your corn, unyoke your oxen, provided only that you send us mushrooms."

The first cultivated mushrooms appeared around 1600 A.D. in limestone caves outside of Paris, thus introducing them to Europe. During the reign of King Louis XIV (1638–1715) mushrooms were cultivated and became a big industry. In America they were grown in cellars, limestone or sand caves, cisterns, and under greenhouse benches. By the late 1800s, mushrooms were a thriving industry.

Here are some tips for the purchase, care, and storage of mushrooms:

• Look for clear, unblemished surfaces and caps tightly closed over the stems.

• Plan to eat them soon after purchase. Store them at about 55° F. with a relative humidity of 85 percent to 90 percent for no more than five days.

• To clean, wipe mushrooms with a damp cloth. Or jiggle them up and down briefly in cool water and then blot dry. Or just rinse quickly under cool running water and then dry immediately and thoroughly.

• To cook mushrooms, three to five minutes are long enough. Mushrooms are little sponges so they soak up the essence of whatever they're cooked in. The more you slice them up, the more flavor they absorb.

• To cook, bring a few tablespoons of liquid to a boil in a saucepan. Add mushrooms; cover. Let simmer for five minutes. Season with desired herbs and spices.

Mushrooms contribute a meatlike flavor and color to sauces and gravies. Like to dry your own? Here's how:

1. All you need is plenty of mushrooms, a large mesh screen, and about four days of sunny, dry summer weather.

2. Just wipe the mushrooms off and slice them paper thin. This is easy to do if the mushrooms are very fresh.

3. Spread them out in one layer on the screen which has been supported on sawhorses or chairs three or four feet off the ground, so that air circulates freely around them.

4. Dry in the sun, turning occasionally, until they are light brown and moisture free. If the drying takes more than a day, bring the mushrooms inside overnight.

5. Drying will take anywhere from one to four days, depending upon the dryness of the air and the thickness of the mushrooms. When they are perfectly dry, store them in a cool, dry place. Mushrooms can also be frozen. Just wipe them clean, sauté in butter, and cool to room temperature. Put enough for one recipe into a freezer container and freeze. Do not use plastic bags or the mushrooms will pick up the flavor of the plastic. Dried mush-

rooms are 44 percent protein. Use one-and-a-half ounces of chips to equal one pound of fresh.

BROCCOLI

For a vegetable that's head and shoulders above the rest, try broccoli. It ranks first in nutrient concentration of ten major vitamins and minerals, seventh in nutrients per calorie, and there are only 26 calories in a cup.

This cousin to the cabbage and twin to cauliflower is *choux broccoli*—"cabbage broccoli" to Frenchmen—but the name is Italian and means "little sprouts." It has long been a favorite among Italians, who found out about it at Caesar's orgies. Catherine de Medicis introduced broccoli to the French in 1533, as a sort of bonus in her bride's dowry. Farmers who have been cultivating it between the olive and fruit trees in their Campania *Felix* (fortunate country) near Naples brought it to America a hundred years ago. The flavor and crispness of U.S. varieties is now world renowned.

Broccoli also has twice as much vitamin C (135 milligrams) as an orange; almost as much calcium as whole milk (88 milligrams per two-thirds cup); 2,500 I.U. of vitamin A; and places first as a vegetable source of B_2, plus phosphorus; 1.2 milligrams iron; 125 milligrams B_1; 1.2 milligrams niacin; 36 milligrams magnesium; and traces of iodine.

Broccoli is best when dark green, with no open flowers, yellowing, or wilted leaves—all of which indicate aging. And its supply of potassium (400 milligrams) aids against water retention. Broccoli is a good source of vitamin A (2,500 I.U.), for instance, which is essential during pregnancy and breast feeding and aids growth, eyesight, and healthy skin.

Store your broccoli under high humidity and low temperatures. Wash well and wrap in foil.

Trick of the trade: Want to create your own broccoli flowers like those professional chefs do? It's really simple, and the satisfaction is much greater than the effort involved. You cut broccoli stalks into two-and-a-half-inch lengths; peel. Lay them on a chopping board and slice downward, s-l-o-w-l-y, leaving them joined at one end, into quarter-inch slices. Half turn the stalk so it lies flat. Cut into narrower strips, keeping them joined at one end. Soak in ice water until the cut ends curl.

SPINACH

Spinach. How sweet it is. Of the ten vegetables that provide the most for your nutrition dollar, only two—carrots and spinach—appear on the average American's vegetable hit parade.

Of America's thirty-nine best-liked vegetables in terms of overall nutrition, spinach is number two. But it's number one in hemoglobin boosting iron, number two in calcium (167 milligrams) and riboflavin (B_2), number three in potassium and vitamin A (14,500 units—twice as high as kale and beet greens), ranks with brewer's yeast as a source of folic acid, and contains almost two dozen of those mighty mini-nutrients known as trace minerals. All this for only 28 calories per half cup.

Spinach originated in Persia and was unknown in Europe until the Moorish invasion of Spain. In the sixteenth century, greens fanciers were still referring to what we now think of as Popeye's favorite vegetable as the "Spanish Vegetable."

Use it or you'll lose it is no joke when it comes to this jolly green giant of nutrition. Unlike fresh greens that don't lose more than 10 percent of their A.A., frozen spinach has a nutrient loss of 29 percent at room temperature in twenty-four hours, 63 percent when refrigerated, and 35 percent when frozen for a week. Fresh spinach has twice as much magnesium after it's cooked; more than half again as much protein; more calcium, phosphorus, iron, sodium, and potassium; more vitamin A, thiamine, riboflavin, and niacin; and almost four times more vitamin C!

THE ONION

Onions and garlic are sisters under the skin. From the elegant leek to the elephant garlic, all the alliums may be "stinkers" but they treat us like family—battling our colds, flavoring our sauces, lowering our cholesterol,* and providing us with an alternative to

* See Chapter VIII, The Carrot Chest: Vegetable Remedies.

salt that's as good as they come while adding fewer than 50 calories per serving to our diets.

As a tasty, healthful vegetable for eating, onions—raw or cooked—are said to improve kidney function and speed the excretion of urine. This factor, combined with their low sodium content, gives them importance in the treatment of heart-circulation problems.

Onions originated in the Far East, became a dietary staple in ancient Egypt and the Mediterranean, and were introduced to the Western world by Spanish explorers. This food has been popular here ever since. Average per capita consumption of onions—fresh, dehydrated, canned, and frozen—is about 13 pounds a year, and annual production runs around 3.3 billion pounds, bringing farmers an estimated $237 million yearly.

The leading producer, California, grows 30 percent of the nation's annual crop, marketing fresh onions every month of the year. Texas accounts for about 16 percent of our supply, and Colorado leads in production of "pearl" onions.

Commercially, onions are classified by type—globe, Spanish, and grano-granex—and color. Globes are grown mostly in the Midwest and East, but are unsuitable to southern climates. The strongly flavored globes keep well under storage. Spanish onions, primarily grown in western states under irrigation, have a sweet flavor and poor storage ability. Mild grano and granex onions are grown largely in southern and southeastern areas. Leeks are sweeter than other types, shallots are mild.

According to USDA, onions contain about 172 calories per pound raw and 132 calories per pound cooked (one medium onion has 38 calories, five green onions about 45). They contain the minerals calcium, phosphorus, and iron, and vitamins A and C plus B vitamins thiamine, riboflavin, and niacin.

And onions are always there when we need them. Emergency onion juice? Just take one slice from a yellow onion, sprinkle with salt, and scrape with a sharp knife and your onion will weep.

As a snack, onions are delicious just as is, sliced, served raw and very cold with plenty of ground pepper and good basil.

And true to the core, onions pay you back in kind. One pound of sets should produce fifty feet of plants. Pull the young ones for green onion eating, and let the others mature. If you have one hundred days to wait, you can grow them from seed.

Garlic?

One hundred grams of this good herb supplies calories (137), fat (.2 grams), phosphorus (202 milligrams), iron (1.5 milligrams), potassium (529 milligrams), niacin (.5 milligrams), and vitamin C (15 milligrams).

U.S. producers grind out almost as much garlic as they do pepper—200 million pounds a year (two-thirds of it dehydrated).

Garlic is native to the Mediterranean and there is an inscription on the Great Pyramid of Giza (built in 3000 B.C.) giving the exact cost of garlic, radishes, and onions consumed during construction.

Garlic's nutrients are similar to onions, and similarly it is as potent a medicinal as it is a culinary. The active part of garlic is the essential oil, a combination of sulphur-containing compounds believed to lower or stabilize cholesterol levels.

It should be stored in a capped jar and kept in a cool cupboard.

III

Carrot Tips: Tricks for Getting Thinner

A man or woman on a diet is a desperate person. He or she clutches at straws, grapefruits, sugar-free soda, biofeedback, black coffee—anything that gets the job done. Or seems to.

After all, it must have been *something* we ate that did it. So (we reason) it'll be something we eat that *undoes* it. And when all else fails? Some of us even have our jaws wired shut.

But why go that far? Little things can mean a lot if you have a little or a lot to lose. If you're already suffering no-macaroni shell shock, why do you need the support of extra tricks, too? Because "there are some strong-willed people who can lose weight on their own," says one weight specialist, Dr. Dale G. Friend, of Harvard Medical School, "but most of the human race do not have that kind of willpower." Too true.

There's always another trick for getting thinner you haven't heard. So here are a few well-chosen "losing" propositions to consider:

1. Get a *diet diary* going. You're less likely to eat too much if you know you'll have to "eat and tell."

2. Hungry? Don't eat and run. Just run. Exercise burns calories,

43

raises blood sugar levels, takes your attention off food, and improves your self-image.

3. Can't let those leftovers be? Pop them in little freezer cartons (instead of your mouth), label, and refrigerate. When you've saved enough, make soup.

4. Cheery thought number 1: If you eat one cup of *green* beans instead of one cup of *baked* beans, you save 290 calories!

5. A one-egg omelet that looks like two? Combine one egg with one tablespoon of milk or water. Scramble on one side only, then place under the broiler to puff it up. Or, make bigger omelets with smaller calorie counts by folding two whipped egg whites into one yolk.

6. Dieters' stew for dinner: Replace half the ground beef in any stew, stir-fry, or burger recipe with fresh ground mushrooms, and do your sautéeing in a heavy skillet rubbed with just enough oil to prevent sticking and burning.

7. If you have to shop for such things as cake, along with cookies, pastries, and ice cream, make sure you buy them in only the flavors and fillings you hate.

8. If walking softly and carrying a carrot stick doesn't do it, try stopping a snack attack with acupressure. Insert the tips of your index fingers gently into your ears, the palms of your hands facing outward. Do not insert your fingers deep into the ear canals themselves. Now place your thumbs on the outer part of your ears, immediately in front of your index fingers. They should be resting on the small lobes to the front of your ears, not the large lobes at the bottom of your ears. Now massage the small lobes firmly between your thumbs and index fingers for at least one minute. This technique should make you feel less hungry 75 percent of the time.

9. Nuts to nuts. What's better than calorie-rich goobers? Fill your snack bowl with raw fresh peas.

10. The saltine alternative: fat slices of fresh raw zucchini spread with low-calorie mayonnaise or yogurt.

11. Serve a 10-calorie "rutabagel" instead of a 200-calorie cheese spread. Slice raw rutabagas and using a pineapple cutter, cut into mock bagel halves.

12. Fat chances: 100 extra calories a day adds up to ten pounds at the end of a year. But not if you take a fifteen-minute walk a

day, or jump five minutes. In fact, thirty minutes of brisk locomotion can keep off or take off as much as twenty-six pounds a year.

13. Need a little obedience training for a runaway appetite? Try sugar-free herbal ice cubes made from any leftover tea. For looks, freeze an edible leaf or flower inside. Keep a sack of cubes in your freezer for emergencies.

14. Do you brake for doughnuts? Don't. Instead try these fat-free sweets. A handful of partially thawed frozen raisins are iron-rich caramel taste-alikes. And a frozen, slightly thawed ripe banana tastes almost like French vanilla ice cream.

15. Starved? Five'll get you ten it's 3:00 P.M. According to Lois Lindauer, director of the Diet Workshop Chain, the hardest time to stay on a diet is from 3:00 to 6:00 P.M. And the worst social situation for dieters? Restaurants, holidays, and vacations.

16. A single piece of pecan pie with a little whipped cream has more calories and fat than a whole meal including soup, salad, olives, and two hard-boiled eggs. Such a meal also gives you more fiber, vitamins, minerals, and satiety value.

17. Got a bad craving? That ain't good. But it can be remedied. Try coloring your favorite binge food blue or green. (Use harmless natural food coloring derived from beets, or spinach or parsley.) The Mayo Clinic's Dr. Edwin Byard, Jr., says there's nothing like it for turning off the taste buds.

18. Slow down your eating—and your tendency to "shovel it in" by eating with your opposite hand and/or trading your usual silverware for a pair of chopsticks. Wearing a surgeon's mask while fixing other folks' meals may be a deterrent, too.

19. When you're having more than one, make it water. If you drink two cups of sparkling mineral water a day instead of soda, by year's end you'll weigh sixteen pounds less.

20. Want to be a shadow of your present self? Make less seem like more: Serve food in a shell to make portions appear larger: salads in a papaya or avocado half, zucchini boats for meats, scallop shells or ramekins for seafood salads.

Make more of raw snacks: Cut squash on the bias, slice brussels sprouts, snip green beans into several pieces, sliver carrots.

Give salads extra chew appeal: Add a crisp lettuce like romaine, slivered peppers (which are rich in vitamins), crunchy sprouts, apple slices.

21. Is your shape out of shape, or isn't it? Experts say there are two ways you can tell if you've gone past your stop, fatwise. Extra weight settles first in the thighs and hips. And when it settles in your face, hands, and ankles, it's definitely time to turn in the chip and dip.

22. Hunger got you by the bear claws? Put a hold on that sugar craving by taking a big dose of ascorbic acid (500 to 1,000 milligrams) plus a manganese supplement (a trace mineral: best source is blueberries). And skip the 100 calories of honey in your tea, too. Instead, for sweetening try a wedge of orange with tea, iced or hot.

23. Having trouble bellying up to the salad bar? Simply eating more selectively will guarantee you lose weight. For example, one pat of butter less each day for a year, five-and-a-half pounds lost; two teaspoons of sugar less each day, four-and-a-half pounds lost; one twelve-ounce can of beer four times a week, eleven pounds lost; one twelve-ounce soft drink four times a week, four-and-a-half pounds lost; ten potato chips four times a week, six-and-a-half pounds lost; two mixed cocktails each day, six pounds.

24. Anything nontoxic is worth a shot if you've got more than five pounds to lose. Eating backwards, for instance, a bowl of iceburg lettuce rather than a bowl of vanilla ice cream for dessert helps sidetrack your eating momentum. High-fiber food—breads and nuts—do the job, too. They clean the palate and wipe away stronger flavors that cause you to eat more. Or, reach for a cup of unsweetened herb tea instead of a sweet cookie.

25. Live one low-calorie day at a time. A good, high-protein snack when you're running on empty? "Squeegies." Slice a block of tofu, marinate overnight in oil and soy sauce; drain. Freeze. Thaw or steam; squeeze dry. Only 150 tiny calories in eight big ounces.

26. Like to make less of yourself? Make more butterless sauces with yogurt. It decalorizes, blends flavors, and adds a tanginess of its own. For sauce: simmer a little white wine, then swirl in yogurt, but don't boil. Pour on patties, steamed vegetables. 2) For salads: Shake up three tablespoons yogurt, one tablespoon oil, vinegar, mustard, and pepper. Toss with greens.

27. Chew a few. Stew a few. Raw foods are a real crutch. They're more filling than cooked equivalents, 30 percent richer nutritionally, and sometimes lower in calories.

IV

Uncommon Facts about Common Garden Variety Vegetables

• Eat greens to stay in the pink. It takes seventeen bowls of salad to do the calorie damage of one piece of chocolate Bavarian cream pie

• Intelligence for the home gardener: Beans thrive best interplanted with carrots or beets. And radishes, cukes, corn, or turnips will grow well if you're raising a plot of peas (but mix in the onions, garlic, and shallots).

• The body absorbs over seventeen percent of the pro-vitamin carotene (from which vitamin A is formed) in raw carrots, 20 percent in cooked carrots, but nearly all of the carotene (along with minerals, enzymes, and other nutrients) when carrots are freshly juiced.

• One pound of boiled newly harvested potatoes deliver a full day's requirement of vitamin C. One medium-size white potato has 80 calories (no more than a medium-size apple); potatoes are more easily digested than any other vegetable.

• Dandelion greens contain more vitamin A than carrots, more iron than beefsteak, and nearly as much calcium as milk.

47

• The usual half-cup serving of most vegetables contains only 50 calories (starchier types average twice as much).

• Red bell peppers have more vitamin C than green peppers and four times more vitamin C than oranges.

• Consumer beware: Fresh vegetables liable to be waxed include: carrots, parsnips, cucumbers, bell peppers, tomatoes, eggplants, potatoes, rutabagas (along with wax, coloring matter may also be added to the surface). An in-store sign should, but often does not, announce this fact.

• Research studies by Russian scientists indicate that onions are a valuable preventive medicine in the treatment of atherosclerosis and high blood pressure. Onions are rich in calcium, phosphorus, potassium, and vitamin A and contain strong germ-killing biochemicals. Low in sodium, and low in calories, they are also a mild natural diuretic.

• The roots of the caraway plant are edible and taste like carrots.

• There is more food value in two large sprigs of parsley than there is in a whole plateful of iceberg lettuce: A half cup (four ounces) of chopped fresh parsley has approximately 10,000 units of vitamin A, almost 200 milligrams of vitamin C (more than a similar amount of oranges); several B vitamins; and generous amounts of calcium, iron, phosphorus, and potassium.

• For low-calorie, high-quality nutrient-rich water nothing beats fresh fruits and vegetables. Raw cauliflower is 91 percent water, carrots 88.2 percent, cabbage 92.4 percent, and even "dry" onions are 89.1 percent.

• Spinach may not give you muscles, but it'll supply you with at least thirty minerals and trace elements. The green stuff contains potassium, calcium, phosphorus, bromine, aluminum, thorium, manganese, strontium, rubidium, copper, chromium, lanthanum, scandium, antimony, thallium, mercury, nickel, europium, arsenic, lead, cobalt, cadmium, nitrogen, uranium, boron, iron, zinc, carbon, hydrogen, and oxygen, says the *Environmental Engineering News.*

• Eating foods from the nightshade family, says Norman Childers, horticulturist at Rutgers University, is a significant causative factor in arthritis. If you suffer from arthritis, try a vegetable fast. That means no more tomatoes, potatoes, or eggplant.

• How about a little potato prestidigitation? Leave a potato at room temperature too long—over a week—and the potato starch will turn to sugar, and you will then have a sweet potato substitute.

• Fresh vegetables contain 96 percent more vitamin E than commercial processed counterparts.

• Better a little broccoli than a lot: According to the magazine *Let's Live*, rutabaga, turnip, kale, cabbage, cauliflower, brussel sprouts, and broccoli all contain the chemical 1.5-vinyl-2-Thiooxazolidine which acts as a thyroid depressant. And parsnips contain myristicin, an insecticidal component deadly to fruit flies, Mexican bean beetles, and mosquito larvae. (The quantities are minute enough to make them safe eating.)

• Eat your nettle. Why? Because it contains lots of leafy green alpha tocopherol (98.2 I.U.), otherwise known as vitamin E, one of the reasons you start your day with wheat germ. So does cabbage (40.7), mint (33.8), and spinach (17.0). The RDA is 15 I.U.

• Did you eat your eight-and-a-half pounds per capita share of pickled cucumbers this year? You should. The vitamin-A content of cucumbers is increased during the pickling process. Cukes have enough vitamin C, long evidenced by the pickle's place on ships, to make them an antiscurvy food; and they are easily digested, because of the various acids they contain.

• Your favorite vegetable may actually be a fruit, botanically speaking, if it's a tomato, cucumber, pepper, eggplant, or an orange-fleshed squash.

V
A Week of Menus

An asterisk (*) means see Chapter VII, "The Recipes."

SEVEN BREAKFASTS

1.

> 1 cup carrot-apple Reducer Juicer,* or 1 cup salt-free
>   bouillon
> handful raw sunflower seeds
> Anise Celery Sticks *

Less than 350 calories

2.

> Herb tea with orange wedge
> ½ cup steamed millet with 1 teaspoon each honey and raw
>   wheat germ
> 1 small ripe banana

Less than 300 calories

3.

½ grapefruit or ½ cup grapefuit juice
1 thin piece cinnamon toast
½ ounce Cheddar cheese or Tofu Bacon *

                                   Less than 350 calories

4.

1 cup Big Red *
unsalted melba toast
1 Taster's Choice Muffin *

                                   Less than 400 calories

5.

1 cup carrot-coconut Reducer Juicer *
2 Carrot Cake Cookies *
handful of raw nuts or sprouts

                                   Less than 400 calories

6.

½ cup steamed millet with ½ cup yogurt
1 cup strawberries, cherries, or dried peaches

                                   Less than 300 calories

7.

4 ounces tofu brushed with 1 teaspoon each honey and oil,
   broiled
1 small bran muffin
herb tea or coffee

                                   Less than 300 calories

SEVEN LUNCHES

1.

> 2 Salad Bars *
> 4 ounces broiled tofu
> ½ cup raw spinach leaves
> Vitamin Dressing *
> 1 medium tangerine, pear, or apple

Less than 350 calories

2.

> 1 slice 20 Carrots Bread I *
> 1 cup Great Gratings * salad
> herb tea
> 1 small sugar-free cookie

Less than 300 calories

3.

> 1 cup herb coffee (Pero, Postum)
> ½ avocado filled with alfalfa sprouts
> Ultimato Salad Dressing *
> ½ cup mushrooms broiled with 1 teaspoon oil

Less than 300 calories

4.

> ½ cup Cheese-free Camembert *
> 4 whole grain wafers or ½ cup plain yogurt with one
>   tablespoon toasted wheat germ
> 1 cup Herbal Slim *

Less than 400 calories

5.

¼ cup Mock Mayo I *
1 cup raw cauliflower, broccoli buds, radish sticks, carrot
   sticks
½ cup Mock Split Pea Soup,* or B-8 Juice (see p. 156)
Wheat thins

Less than 350 calories

6.

½ cup Broth *
Mock Mayo *
1 tomato, sliced
2 handfuls raw almonds

Less than 350 calories

7.

1 baked potato, or ½ cup Perfect Brown Rice *
½ cup cottage cheese
½ orange, sliced

Less than 300 calories

SEVEN DINNERS

1.

1 cup 20 Carrots Tofu *
1 cup raw spinach or shredded cabbage
1 tablespoon each lemon juice and vegetable oil
1 small wedge 20 Carrots Cake *
1 teaspoon Tofu Whipped Cream *

Less than 300 calories

2.

1 cup zucchini cut into "spaghetti" slivers
lemon juice and warm vegetable oil
handful of raw carrot sticks
1 tangerine
1 pear or 1 cup fresh strawberries
herb tea

                                        Less than 300 calories

3.

1 cup Vegetarian Stroganoff *
1 cup Great Gratings *
sparkling mineral water with sliced lime

                                        Less than 300 calories

4.

4 small Mung Foo Yung * pancakes
1 cup tossed salad
mustard and yogurt dressing (½ teaspoon mustard to 1 cup
    yogurt)
herb tea or Sanka

                                        Less than 350 calories

5.

Mock Salmon Loaf * with rice wafers
½ cup Greens and Grains * (Cream of Spinach and
    Buckwheat Soup)
1 cup chopped unsweetened fruit or berries

                                        Less than 450 calories

6.

1 cup vegetable juice
1 serving Broiler Maker Bean Curd *
½ cup steamed rice or millet
½ grapefruit, sliced, raw or broiled

Less than 400 calories

7.

1 serving Green Pea Soufflé *
1 cup any raw greens (chard, spinach, dandelions, beets,
    etc.)
2 tablespoons oil, 1 tablespoon mild vinegar, and kelp
    dressing
herb coffee
1 Potato Candy * ball
sparkling mineral water

Less than 400 calories

VI

One Potato, Two Potato: Ingredient Guidelines

SHOPPING SAVVY

1. Look for the words *natural, raw, unfiltered, unrefined, whole grain, low sodium, unsweetened, unpasteurized,* and so on. What you see may not be always what you get but it'll be better than the competition.

This also means you should opt for "whole" foods, such as whole wheat, peanuts *with* skins, undegerminated corn, et cetera, that have been freshly ground (i.e., flour, peanut butter), freshly picked, or as freshly packed as possible. Look for unrefined oils sold in cans or dark bottles.

2. Remember, locally harvested honey is healthier for you; so are dairy products produced by hometown hens and cows. Ditto freshly ground flour, just-processed nut butters, and tofu from a neighborhood soycrafter. If your health food store offers these services (many do but don't announce it), take advantage of them.

3. Buy organic as often as your budget allows, especially foods

57

you intend to eat without peeling. Even "fresh" foods are heavily sprayed, colored, waxed, and adulterated these days for a variety of reasons. Some of these adulterants are highly toxic, none are innocuous, and they add to the chemical burden your body must cope with. They also speed up the aging process. On the other hand, save a buck on thick-skinned foods such as bananas, coconuts, and pineapples, whose outer skins are destined for disposal anyhow.

4. Avoid salt. You need no more than one gram of sodium a day. Two is pushing it. So high-flavor, low-sodium herbs and spices are your friends on a reducing diet. Per teaspoon, there are only two-tenths of a milligram in black pepper, pure chili powder, and nutmeg.

The only spices that contain one milligram (a most negligible amount) of sodium are allspice, curry powder, fennel, mace, marjoram, tarragon, and thyme. Only four exceed two milligrams: celery seeds, cloves, parsley flakes, and cumin.

Other good choices include seaweed, such as kelp or dulse. Better yet, try sodium ascorbate powder or calcium ascorbate powder. Both add large amounts of vitamin C to your diet while contributing a slightly salty taste to foods. At the very least, buy a good "vegetable salt" or make your own salt-free salt (pp. 60–61).

5. Avoid sugar. It's our most infamous empty calorie food. Keep it off your shelf to avoid temptation.

Use natural sweeteners such as honey, maple syrup, sorghum, rice syrup, date sugar, and molasses, but only in moderation. They stimulate the appetite, contribute plenty of calories, and add nothing four-star nutritionally to your diet.

6. Tout a sprout. One fully packed cup of sprouts (mung, alfalfa, radish) contains about 16 calories. Eaten raw, stir-fried, or steamed, they taste delicious without rice, sauces, gravies, or starches. Sprouts satisfy your protein needs without surplus calories usually associated with most protein-rich foods. Soybeans, peas and lentils (extremely high in protein) are only slightly more in calories than the other sprouts (about 65 calories per cup). But the yield of protein, weight for weight, is aproximately twice that of meat and, in the case of soybeans, four times that of eggs. Sprout flavors and textures are extremely varied too.

Some raw sprouts, such as soy, have the fresh taste of just-picked garden peas. Steamed, the taste changes to a nutty crispness. Other sprouts, such as wheat, rye, and barley are sweet enough to satisfy a craving for something sugary. Rye sprouts are often mistaken for wild rice, especially in soup and rice combinations. Fenugreek sprouts go well with curries, and sprouted sunflowers and lentils add a peppery tang to salads.

The flavors of sprouts change considerably in combination with one another, when cooked in sauces and gravies, and when used in different recipes. The sprouting process also reduces the flatulence potential of beans.

7. Use your bean. Don't bring home the bacon. Bring home the bacon substitute: tofu. Tofu's only ingredient is soybeans, which not only replaces the bacon you should be forsaking on your diet, but can step in for the cheese, bread, eggs, milk, whipped cream, and more.

Nutritionally, eight ounces supply more than a quarter of your daily protein needs and only 147 calories. In fact, after mung and soy sprouts, tofu has the lowest ratio of calories to protein of any known plant food. (Comparatively, the same amount of beef has four-and-a-half times as many calories; an equal weight of eggs has three times as many calories.) As a small bonus, a half pound of tofu supplies 38 percent of an adult's daily calcium requirement and is a good source of iron, potassium, phosphorus, sodium, B vitamins, and vitamin E.

Tofu can be eaten hot, cold, cooked, or uncooked. It is bland and mild but absorbs an amazing amount of flavor. Uncooked, it can be cut into small cubes and slipped into salads or eaten alone. Broiled, it has a texture almost like meat. Cut into tiny pieces and quickly sautéed, it tastes "scrambled," and when it's cut into cubes and stir-fried, it remains soft and absorbent. Deep-fried tofu can become puffy and crisp, almost like a cruller. When it's mashed or blended it becomes a creamy substance, a natural thickener, and can be used as a substitute for cream, Ricotta cheese, or sour cream, with a loss only in calories.

8. There's air, water, and if you're dieting, there's nutritional yeast (or brewer's yeast). High in nutrients, low in calories, use small amounts of this protein-, mineral-, and B-vitamin rich powder in everything you eat or make, to contribute large amounts of fatigue-fighting anti-aging nutrients to your diet.

9. Whole milk, salt, margarine, and high-sodium bouillon cubes or powders are no-no's even if you've got nothing to lose.

But if you do, here are a few healthy alternatives.

THE SUBSTITUTES

Salt-free Salt I

4 tablespoons instant garlic flakes
4 tablespoons instant minced (dried) onion
3 teaspoons powdered mustard
3 teaspoons kelp or dulse powder
1 scant teaspoon ground ginger
¼ teaspoon cayenne pepper
2 tablespoons dried and finely powdered lemon peel
4 tablespoons mixed dehydrated vegetable flakes
    (optional)

Grind or crush all ingredients and store in spice jars.

NOTE: Add any of these to make a "hotter" version of the above: 1 teaspoon toasted cumin seed; toasted black peppercorn or Szechwan peppercorns; toasted radish seed, fenugreek seed (use those sold for sprouting), or powdered horseradish; and/or a pinch of cinnamon or mace to taste.

Salt-free Salt II

2 teaspoons whole coriander seeds
½ teaspoon whole cumin seeds
½ teaspoon powdered mace
⅙ teaspoon powdered allspice
1 bay leaf, powdered
3 sprigs fresh thyme, or ⅙ teaspoon dry thyme
1 teaspoon whole fenugreek seeds
2 teaspoons powdered turmeric
¼ teaspoon red pepper flakes

Grind together all ingredients in a blender or spice mill for at least five minutes.

Use sparingly. A good curry powder substitute too.

Salt-free Salt III

dried sage
dried basil
dried thyme
dried celery seeds
dried onion
dried parsley
cayenne
garlic
kelp
paprika

Grind or crush all ingredients.

Salt-free Seasoning Paste

½ cup toasted sesame seeds
1 tablespoon brewer's yeast
2 tablespoons minced parsley
2 tablespoons low-sodium soy sauce
1 scallion, minced
2 tablespoons water

Puree all ingredients in a blender. Use to contribute saltiness to anything except desserts.

Garlic "Salt"

Commercial garlic powder is made by drying and grinding dehydrated garlic cloves to a powder. The cloves are first separated by hand and the paperlike outer coating is peeled away before the cloves are dehydrated. At home, you can remove the skin from the sets, or slice them to allow the air to penetrate to the inside of the sets. Carefully dry the cloves and, when completely dry, pound them into a powder. This powder can then be stored and used the same as the commercial variety, although you should check the strength before using.

Carrot-Top "Salt"

Nutritionally, those feathery leaves on top of your carrots are no frippery. They are a good source of nerve-energizing phosphorus and vitamin E. Here's how to turn them into a seasoning powder.

Simply disconnect them and dry them in an oven heated only by the pilot light. This low heat (under 120° F.) doesn't destroy nutrients. If you don't have a gas stove, just turn your electric oven to warm, then turn it off before putting in the greens. Or dry the greens out in the sun, carefully protected from insects.

In about twenty-four hours the greens become very dry and brittle. Crush them and put the powder into a shaker-top container. (A whole basketful of greens hardly fills a salt shaker.)

Sprinkle the powder over soups, salads, and casseroles—just about anything. Another nutrition-oriented solution to sodium: Try ascorbate powder, which is a low-sodium form of vitamin C.

Pepper Plus

> ¼ cup black peppercorns
> ¼ cup white peppercorns
> 2 tablespoons whole allspice

Combine. Funnel into mill. Use in place of black pepper in any recipe.

Or, how about:

Pepper Minus

> ¼ cup mustard, poppy, caraway, sesame, or dill seeds
> ¾ cup peppercorns

Use an old pepper mill to grind ingredients. You can also use half-and-half proportions.

Use when you want a subtle hint of pepper with an herbal accent.

Instant Soup Cubes

Super bouillon.

> 3 cups tightly packed fresh coriander, parsley, watercress,
>   or spinach leaves
> 2 cups cold water

Puree in blender.
Freeze in cubes.
Transfer cubes to a large plastic bag in freezer. One cube equals 2 tablespoons chopped greens in any recipe (except salads) where fresh leaves are essential.
VARIATION: For high-protein soup cubes, add 1 tablespoon brewer's yeast before blending.

Broth Powder

> 3 parts mixed dried vegetable flakes
> 1 part salt-free salt

Mix and grind or crush a small amount at a time, when needed. Spices and herbs begin losing their potency under the best of conditions in a few weeks.
To use, dilute with plain water, nutrient-rich water saved from steaming vegetables, or water used to soak seeds for sprouting. Or use "straight" as a seasoning.
NOTE: Low-sodium, all-vegetable broth powders and flakes are also available at most health food stores.

Nature's Butter I

The margarine alternative.

> 6 tablespoons sweet butter, softened
> ¼ cup safflower oil
> ¼ cup plain yogurt or buttermilk

Using an electric mixer, blend ingredients.
Put in a 1-cup container tub.
Refrigerate until spreadable. It will yield a better butter that's higher in polyunsaturated fats, lower in calories and sodium, and deliciously homemade. About 75 calories per tablespoon.

Nature's Butter II

> *1 cup safflower, soy, or corn oil*
> *1 cup sweet, softened butter*
> *2 tablespoons water*
> *2 tablespoons dried skim milk*
> *¼ teaspoon lecithin*

Blend all ingredients until smooth.

Pour into containers and store in refrigerator.

VARIATION: Want a 20 Carrots Butter? Add a few drops of pure carrot juice to the finished product. About 50 calories per tablespoon.

Vegetable Milk

No-fat, no-cholesterol mock milk with only 50 calories a cup.

> *2 small zucchini*

Peel zucchini and cut into one-inch chunks.

Fill blender ¼ full. Liquefy until thick and milky. Repeat until all liquefied. Makes 1 cup.

Use in cooked desserts and main dishes in place of skim or whole milk.

VARIATION: Make a low-calorie vegetable milk-and-egg beater. Cover 1 cup bread cubes or crumbs with zucchini milk. Substitute for milk and eggs in meatloaf recipes, et cetera.

WHAT ELSE?

You'll lose more if there's method in your reductive reasoning. Little additions, restrictions, and reductions add up. For instance:

1. Cut calories 75 percent by using 50 percent less oil. How? A heavy pot is your ace in the hole. Then just rub it with enough oil to prevent burning and sauté as usual. If food begins to dry out, add wine or water. Replace lid and steam until done.

Also don't pour oil on your food—sprinkle it from an empty salt shaker so you can monitor and minimize your intake.

2. Raw is best. But steaming can save you hundreds of calories a

day and who knows how many pounds a year. And you can steam anything from pumpkins to popovers. (Yes, even a nonsticky biscuit dough can go into that vegetable steamer for a change of pace.)

THE STEAM TABLE

Vegetable	Steaming Time (minutes)
Artichokes, globe or French, medium, whole	20–25
Artichokes, globe or French, large, whole	30–35
Artichokes, Jerusalem (sunchoke), 2 ounces each, peeled, whole	25–30
Asparagus, medium stalks, whole	4–5
Beans, green or wax, whole	6–7
Beets, medium, whole	25–30
Broccoli, separated into flowerets with stems, sliced ⅜-inch thick	5–6
Brussels sprouts, medium, whole	8
Cabbage, green, 1½ pounds, quartered	15
Carrots, medium (4 ounces each), whole	14
Carrots, thinly sliced (with food processor)	4
Cauliflower, 1½ pounds, whole	12
Cauliflower, separated into flowerets	7–9
Corn, freshly shucked, whole	4–6
Eggplant, 1 pound, halved lengthwise	12
Endive, Belgian, halved lengthwise	4–5
Leeks, medium, halved lengthwise	6–7
Mushrooms, sliced ¼-inch thick, placed in heat-proof bowl	4
Onions, small (1½-inch diameter), whole	10
Parsnips, peeled, halved lengthwise	16–18
Peas, green, shelled, placed in heat-proof bowl	4–6
Potatoes, new, red-skinned, small, whole	15–20
Potatoes, sweet, or yams, peeled and cubed	20–25
Potatoes, sweet, or yams, 9 ounces each, whole	30–35
Spinach, leaves torn, destemmed	4–6
Squash, acorn, 1½ pounds, halved	20–25
Squash, butternut, 1½ pounds, halved	20–25
Squash, zucchini or yellow summer, 1½-inches diameter, whole	7
Squash, zucchini or yellow summer, sliced ½-inch thick	4
Turnips, white, medium (3 ounces each), whole	25–30

3. To add protein to any meal, add cheese, seeds, nuts, a glass of milk, brewer's yeast.

To add calcium to any meal, add cheese, yogurt, or milk.

To add iron to any meal, add seeds, nuts, deep green leafy salads, eggs, wheat germ.

To add vitamin A to any meal, add carrots, apricots, deep green leafy salads.

To add B vitamins to any meal, add seeds, nuts, brewer's yeast, wheat germ, cheese, milk.

To add vitamin C to any meal, add fresh fruit or green leafy vegetables.

4. Are you a nut nut? There are easily over three hundred kinds growing. Maximize the nutrition you get by shelling nuts yourself. Here's what to expect:

Almonds		
unblanched, whole	6⅓ ounces	1¼ cups
blanched, slivered	4½ ounces	1 cup
Brazil nuts, whole	7⅔ ounces	1½ cups
Cashews, whole	4½ ounces	1 cup
Peanuts, whole, roasted	11⅔ ounces	2⅓ cups
Pecans, halves	8½ ounces	2¼ cups
Walnuts, halves	7¼ ounces	2 cups

MEASURE FOR MEASURE

Equivalents

Dash or pinch equals less than ⅛ teaspoon
3 teaspoons equal 1 tablespoon
2 tablespoons equal ⅛ cup
4 tablespoons equal ¼ cup
5 tablespoons plus 1 teaspoon equal ⅓ cup
8 tablespoons equal ½ cup
10 tablespoons plus 2 teaspoons equal ⅔ cup
12 tablespoons equal ¾ cup
16 tablespoons equal 1 cup
1 cup equals 8 fluid ounces
2 cups equal 1 pint (16 fluid ounces)
2 pints equal 1 quart (32 fluid ounces)
1 quart equals 4 cups
4 quarts equal 1 gallon
16 ounces (dry measure) equal 1 pound

METRIC WEIGHTS

Dry Measure

Convert known ounces into grams by multiplying by 28
Convert known pounds into kilograms by multiplying by .45
Convert known grams into ounces by multiplying by .035
Convert known kilograms into pounds by multiplying by 2.2

Liquid Measure

Convert known ounces into milliliters by multiplying by 30
Convert known pints into liters by multiplying by .47
Convert known quarts into liters by multiplying by .95
Convert known gallons into liters by multiplying by 3.8
Convert known milliliters into ounces by multiplying by .034

MORE SUBSTITUTIONS

1 tablespoon arrowroot flour or cornstarch equals 2 tablespoons regular flour
1 teaspoon baking powder equals ¼ teaspoon baking soda plus ½ teaspoon cream of tartar, or ¼ teaspoon baking soda plus ½ cup buttermilk, or ¼ teaspoon baking soda plus ⅓ cup molasses
1 tablespoon potato flour equals 2 tablespoons regular flour, or 1 tablespoon starch
1 tablespoon flour equals 1½ teaspoons cornstarch, or ¾ tablespoon quick-cooking tapioca
1 cup unbleached white flour equals 1 cup cornmeal
1 cup sifted all-purpose flour equals 1⅛ cups (1 cup plus 2 tablespoons) sifted cake flour
1 cup cream equals ⅓ cup powdered milk and ½ cup water, or 3 tablespoons butter plus ¾ cup milk, or ⅓ cup butter plus ¾ cup milk
1 cup fresh milk equals ½ cup evaporated milk plus ½ cup water (also reduce the sugar in the recipe), or 4 tablespoons powdered skim milk, 2 tablespoons butter, and 1 cup water
2 egg yolks equal 1 whole egg (whole eggs can be substituted)
1 cup honey equals 1–1¼ cups sugar plus ¼ cup liquid; ½ cup honey equals ¾ cup sugar plus ⅛ cup liquid

1 cup yogurt equals 1 cup buttermilk, or 1 cup sour cream
½-1½ teaspoons dry herbs equal 1 tablespoon fresh herbs
⅛ teaspoon garlic powder equals 1 small clove fresh garlic

OVEN TEMPERATURES

Oven temperatures are described as slow, moderate, hot, and very hot. How do you know? Here's one way: slow, 250°-300° F.; moderate, 325°-375° F.; hot, 400°-450° F.; very hot, anything over 450° F.

You should have an oven thermometer. But in case you don't, here's an oven test to give you some idea of how hot your oven really is: Sprinkle a teaspoon of flour on a piece of brown paper and put it in the oven at 350° F. If flour browns lightly in five minutes, you have a slow oven. If it turns golden brown in five minutes, it is moderate. If it registers dark brown in five minutes, the oven is hot. In three minutes? The oven is very hot indeed.

VII
The Recipes

Appetizers and Snacks

APPETIZERS

Cheese-free Camembert

2 cups rolled oats
2 tablespoons sunflower seeds (see NOTE *below)*
1 teaspoon celery seeds
1 teaspoon caraway seeds
1 teaspoon dill seed
1 teaspoon soy sauce

Mix all ingredients in a bowl and add cold water to cover. Transfer to wide-mouth jar covered with cheesecloth.

Store for two to three days, until mixture has soured. Use as a dip or spread. Makes 2 cups.

NOTE: If you'd like to start from scratch with your sunflower seeds, here's a time-saving way to shell them: Put 1 cup of seeds at a time in a blender at top speed for about 3 seconds, then dump the contents into a spaghetti blancher filled with cold water. The shells will float on the top while the nutmeats sink to the bottom. The empty shells can be skimmed off with a large slotted spoon. Then just lift up the inner portion of the blancher and allow the excess water to drain off (the holes in the blancher's liner are too small for the seeds to pass through). All you have left to do is dry and roast the nutmeats and store them in jars until you're ready for granola, cookies, or just a good snack.

Less than 50 calories per tablespoon

Hasen Pepper

Quick-pickled peppers: a perfect low-calorie vegetarian substitute for marinated herring.

> 1½ pounds bell peppers, a mix of red and green ones, or
>   use red-green peppers
> whole peppercorns
> 2 tablespoons red wine or rice vinegar
> 4 tablespoons olive oil
> pinch of kelp or Salt-free Salt I, II, or III (see pp. 60–61)
> 1 teaspoon miso (soybean paste),* or soy sauce
> 1 small clove garlic, crushed

Preheat the broiler. Put the whole peppers on a broiler tray and broil about 2 inches from the heat for 15 to 20 minutes, turning them from side to side until they are slightly deflated and the skins are puckered and charred.

Pop them into a paper bag, close, and let rest for 10 minutes until the skins loosen and cool. Peel off the charred skins, core, discard seeds, and cut the peppers into thin strips.

Put in a serving bowl, grinding pepper generously on top.

Mix all the rest of the ingredients together and combine with peppers. Serve immediately or let marinate in the refrigerator overnight. Yields 6 servings.

Less than 75 calories per ½ cup serving

---

* Nonvegetarians may substitute the more traditional anchovy fillets.

Red, White, and Blue Green Peppers

> *8 ounces blue cheese, softened **
> *⅓ cup minced radish*
> *¼ cup snipped chives*
> *5 tablespoons minced parsley*
> *2 tablespoons softened butter*
> *pepper to taste*
> *1 large green pepper, washed*
> *1 large bell pepper, washed*

In a bowl combine well blue cheese, radishes, chives, 3 tablespoons minced parsley, butter, and pepper to taste.

Quarter lengthwise 1 green pepper and 1 red bell pepper and fill the quarters with the cheese mixture. Halve each quarter lengthwise and dip the ends in remaining minced parsley.

Arrange the strips on a platter, alternating the colors, and chill them for 30 minutes. Makes 16 strips.

Less than 50 calories per strip

Anise Celery Sticks

> *1 teaspoon anise extract*
> *1 quart cold water*
> *1 bunch celery, sliced into sticks*

Add anise extract to water. Add celery sticks. Crisp for 4 or more hours before serving.

Less than 25 calories per cupful

* To reduce calories, combine 4 ounces mashed tofu with blue cheese.

Marinated Anise Carrots

8 medium carrots, scraped, sliced diagonally
2 quarts boiling water
1½ teaspoons salt
½ cup olive oil
¼ cup lemon juice
1 tablespoon anise seeds
1 tablespoon white vinegar
¼ teaspoon pepper

Place carrots in saucepan with 2 quarts boiling water and 1 teaspoon salt.

Cook, covered, until crisp-tender, about 3½ minutes. Drain immediately, run under cold water to stop cooking process.

Combine olive oil, lemon juice, anise seeds, vinegar, pepper, and remaining ½ teaspoon salt. Pour over carrots.

Cover and refrigerate overnight. Serve on leaf lettuce, if desired. Makes 3 cups.

Less than 90 calories per ½ cup serving

Horseradish Nasturtium Spread

2 celery stalks
1 tablespoon chopped nasturtium leaves *
1 teaspoon lemon juice
1 teaspoon fresh finely grated horseradish
8 ounces drained yogurt, or cream cheese
whole grain bread or crackers

Wash celery. Coarsely grate. Blend with remaining ingredients in a bowl.

Spread on dark whole-grain bread or crackers. Serve over a bed of whole nasturtium leaves and garnish with nasturtium blossoms.

* Both the leaves and stems of this plant are edible. They have a sweet flavor and a peppery aftertaste like nothing else. They are rich in vitamin C. More, the green seedpods of the nasturtium can be pickled and eaten as a substitute for capers.

VARIATION: See what a scant teaspoon of this puree does for a pot of plain mashed potatoes.

Less than 50 calories per tablespoon

Golden "Boursin"

> 1 pound pot cheese
> 1 clove garlic, mashed
> chopped parsley
> pinch of sage
> pinch of chervil
> pinch of pepper to taste

Mix all ingredients together in a bowl, chill, and use as a dip for celery, carrot sticks, cuke slices, or a spread for toast.
Color with carrot juice or powdered turmeric.

Less than 25 calories per heaping tablespoon

No-Nut "Nut" Butter

> oil or butter
> 5 whole heads of garlic

Preheat oven to 400° F. Oil or butter unpeeled garlic heads and arrange in a heavy skillet.

Place in oven and bake 45 minutes or until cloves are very sweet and tender.

To use as a spread, separate cloves and squeeze the roasted pulp onto your waiting crackers and spread. Ninety percent fewer calories than mayonnaise and cream cheese.

VARIATIONS: Put separated, peeled, oiled garlic cloves in a baking dish. Roast 45 minutes at 250°–275° F. Season without salt. Munch when you're in one of those can't stop after one snack moods.

For a mixed-nut substitute, combine with lightly toasted sprouts, wheat, and a handful of raw nuts. Garlic stabilizes the system, lowers cholesterol, cleanses the body of pollutants, kills germs, and adds lots of antioxidating selenium to your diet, which prevents colds.

Pub Fries

9 large Idaho potatoes, baked
½ cup vegetable oil
brewer's yeast
apple sauce or sour cream

Quarter Idaho potatoes lengthwise while they are still warm and gently scoop out the pulp with a small spoon, leaving the skins intact. Reserve the pulp for another use. Preheat oven to 200° F.

Put 6 potato skins in the basket of a deep fryer, lower the basket slowly into 2 inches of hot vegetable oil (365° F.), and fry the potato skins for 2 minutes, or until they are golden brown.

Drain the skins on paper towels and keep them warm on a platter in a very slow oven. Fry the remaining potato skins and keep them warm in the same manner.

Sprinkle the skins with brewer's yeast and serve them with apple sauce or sour cream.

NOTE: For spatter-free frying, you can use a Dutch oven and a pair of tongs for flipping. Partially cover with a lid to steam-sauté.

Less than 100 calories per fry

Hearts of the East *(Puree of Artichoke)*

6 artichoke hearts, quartered
6 asparagus tips
water to cover
Salt-free Salt I, II, or III (see pp. 60–61)

Poach artichoke hearts and asparagus for about 10 minutes in salted water.

Drain. Puree in a blender. Spread on crackers, warm crepes, or stuff celery stalks. Serves 6.

Less than 15 calories a serving

Carrot-wurst

The cold-cut alternative.

¼ cup finely grated carrot
¼ cup grated beet
¼ cup parsley
¼ cup leek
¼ cup scallion or celery
1 tablespoon crushed caraway seeds
2 ounces almond butter
1 tablespoon grated horseradish, or horseradish cream

In a food processor, by hand, or by hand grater, combine carrot, beet, parsley, leek, scallion or celery, crushed caraway seeds, almond butter, horseradish or horseradish cream.

Knead into a 2-inch by ½-inch roll into long weiner shape on wax paper.

Chill, slice. Use as spread on thin wafers or slices of raw cuke. Yields 10 cocktail servings.

Each serving about 20 calories each

Whip 'n Dip I

2 10-ounce packages frozen small lima beans
2 tablespoons butter
1 teaspoon lemon juice
3 tablespoons or more yogurt, to taste
pepper to taste

In a saucepan put the beans with enough water to cover. Bring to a boil, and simmer 5 minutes. Drain.

Puree the beans in a blender or food processor with the butter, lemon juice, yogurt, and pepper to taste.

VARIATION: Omit lemon juice and pepper. Add Salt-free Seasoning Paste (see p. 61) instead, to taste.

What to dip in the whip? Try raw asparagus cut on the bias; whole green beans, sliced; broccoli flowerets; cauliflower buds; celery sticks; cucumber slices; cantelope sticks; mushroom caps; small whole okra; green onions; green or red pepper slivers; white or red radishes; fresh spinach; cherry tomatoes; zucchini slices.

Less than 30 calories per tablespoon

Whip 'n Dip II

> 2 cups cooked fresh or frozen peas
> 2 tomatoes
> 2 tablespoons soy sauce, or 1 teaspoon Tabasco
> 1 green onion
> garlic powder, or ¼ clove fresh garlic
> Broth Powder (see p. 63)
> kelp

Puree all ingredients together in blender. If too thick, add tomato juice.

Whip 'n Dip II makes a good accompaniment to celery sticks, cucumber slices, or broccoli flowerets.

Less than 40 calories per tablespoon

Mock Chopped Liver I

> 1 medium eggplant
> 1 tablespoon oil
> 1 medium onion, minced
> 2 hard-cooked eggs
> Salt-free Salt or Salt-free Seasoning Paste (see p. 61) to
>   taste

Slice eggplant in ¼-inch circles. Brush with oil and broil * until golden on both sides.

Sauté half of the minced onions. Grind eggplant, both sautéed and raw onions, and eggs in a food grinder or processor. Add "salt" to taste.

Refrigerate. Remove from refrigerator 30 minutes before serving.

Less than 50 calories per heaping tablespoon

* Not for nothing is the eggplant known as "edible blotting paper." Don't brown in the skillet where eggplant soaks up high-calorie oil and butter like a sponge. Broil until brown, turn once, and save calories.

Mock Chopped Liver II

1½ cups cooked chopped green beans
2 hard-cooked eggs, chopped
1 teaspoon brewer's yeast
¼ cup toasted walnuts
1–2 tablespoons Mock Mayo I (see p. 97)
½ cup fine minced onion sautéed in oil or butter
1–2 tablespoons dry wine
Salt-free Salt I, II, or III (see pp. 60–61) and pepper to
  taste
nutmeg

Combine everything in bowl and puree ½ cup at a time. Combine and chill.

Use as a spread or stuffing for tomatoes, celery, green peppers, et cetera. Makes 2 cups.

Less than 50 calories per tablespoon

Snowflakes

1 mature coconut
2 teaspoons soy sauce
1 (or more) teaspoons brewer's yeast

Place whole husked coconut in oven at 500° F. for 15 minutes. Meat will separate from shell.

Crack in half and remove coconut. Slice in strips about 2 inches long and ¼- to ⅛-inch thick. Toss with soy sauce. Place on baking tray.

Toast strips in oven at 250° F. for 45 minutes, stirring occasionally until golden; distribute evenly.

Sprinkle with yeast, stir, and serve. Store extras in an airtight container.

Less than 50 calories per handful

Baked Cantaloupe

1 large ripe cantaloupe
1 teaspoon honey
1 cup herb tea (chamomile or mint)

Preheat oven to 350° F. Slice melon* in half. Baste with honey and tea and place in oven pan. Bake 20 minutes.
Eat warm. Serves 2.

Less than 75 calories per half

Heartless Potatoes I

1 tablespoon melted butter
⅓ cup plain yogurt
¼ teaspoon thyme or basil
4 potatoes, baked
sesame seeds (optional)

Preheat oven to 375° F. In a small dish combine butter, yogurt, and thyme or basil.

Halve the potatoes lengthwise. Leaving about ¼-inch potato next to the skin, scoop the potato meat into a bowl. (Save for mashed potatoes or knishes.)

Brush the insides of the potato skins with the yogurt mixture. Sprinkle with sesame seeds. Place on tray and bake for about 25 minutes. Makes 4 servings.

Less than 50 calories per serving

* Got a biological craving for cantaloupe? It may mean you're deficient in Vitamin A. One quarter of this melon supplies 3,400 I.U. of vitamin A plus vitamin C, calcium, magnesium, and inositol.

Heartless Potatoes II

> *2 Idaho potatoes*
> *olive oil*
> *butter*

Preheat oven to 425° F. Grease potatoes with olive oil and wrap in aluminum foil. Bake for 40 to 60 minutes. When half done, puncture skins with a fork to allow steam to escape. Let cool.

Cut potatoes in half and scoop out meat. Arrange potato skins in an oven-proof serving dish, dab with butter, and reheat. Serve warm. Save the potato meat for the skinny-minny member of the family. Makes 4 servings.

Less than 50 calories per serving

SNACKS

Egg Kraut

A homemade hen's fruit calcium supplement.

> *2 fresh organic eggs*
> *1 jar apple cider vinegar or rice wine vinegar*

Place eggs in a jar of good quality (unpasteurized preferred) apple cider vinegar or rice wine vinegar.

Let "kraut" 8 to 12 hours. Drain and eat, calcium-rich shell and all, for a snack or serve with raw vegetables, salads. Also good in homemade mayos.

Less than 75 calories per egg

Herbal Melba Toast

Lightly butter 2 thin slices of day-old whole-grain bread, sprinkle with chopped marjoram and a pinch of cinnamon. Broil until toasty.

Eggplant Shrinky Dinks

1 large eggplant

Peel and slice a good not-too-seedy, not-too-ripe or mature eggplant into "chips" about ⅛-inch thick. Make chips as uniform as possible.

Process in electric dryer at 140° F. (or drop to 130° F. for the last 60 minutes). Or dry in a 175° F. oven with good ventilation overnight or longer.

Cool chips and store in moisture-proof containers. Serve with Mock Mayo I or II (see p. 97).

VARIATION: Be your own vegetable vending machine. You can use the method above to make your own nearly no-calorie Instant Dried Onion Rings, too. Good for snacks, or in cooked dishes.

Less than 10 calories per chip

Asparagus "Popcorn"

1 bunch fresh asparagus
1 tablespoon sesame oil
ginger root
pinch of Salt-free Salt I, II, or III (see pp. 60–61)
dill or celery seeds

Peel fresh asparagus stalk bottoms. Slice on the extreme bias about ¼ inch thick until you have enough for 3 cups.

Heat sesame oil in a wok or cast-iron skillet. Toss in a few slices of ginger root, add asparagus, and season with Salt-free Salt.

Turn heat up high, cover pan, and agitate pan as you would for corn. Ready in 4 minutes. Sprinkle with warm dill or celery seeds. Serve hot.

Less than 20 calories per half cup

Small Potatoes

Cut calories. Have a bowl of mock macadamia nuts.

> *2 cups tiny new potatoes*
> *oil*
> *brewer's yeast*
> *pepper to taste*
> *pinch of cayenne*

Roast potatoes in a lightly oiled pan, shaking and turning occasionally. When crusty and crunchy, dust with brewer's yeast, pepper, and cayenne.

Less than 150 calories per handful

Nuts to You

> *1 small onion, diced*
> *1 clove garlic, mashed*
> *1 teaspoon freshly grated ginger*
> *1 hot chili, split and seeded*
> *1 teaspoon turmeric*
> *1 cinnamon stick*
> *2 cardamom pods*
> *2 strips lemon rind*
> *Salt-free Salt I, II, or III (see pp. 60–61) to taste*
> *1 cup coconut milk or any vegetable stock*
> *½ pound raw cashews soaked in water overnight*

Combine all ingredients except the cashews in a saucepan and simmer for 10 minutes.

Add the cashews and simmer for 30 minutes, or until the cashews are tender. Add more coconut milk or vegetable stock if too much liquid evaporates.

Makes 4 mini-servings, less than 100 calories each.

Leftovers? Freeze them. They can come forth from your freezer as a good snack when you're stranded in your night kitchen.

Soups, Salads, and Dressings

SOUPS

Broth

> 2 tablespoons oil
> ½ medium onion, chopped
> ½ celery stalk, chopped
> 2 carrots, chopped
> 1 clove garlic, chopped
> 1 small tomato, chopped
> few celery leaves, chopped
> ¼ cup brewer's yeast
> ¼ cup soy sauce
> 3 cups water
> ¼ teaspoon thyme
> ¼ teaspoon basil

Heat oil in skillet. Sauté onion, celery, carrot, and garlic until the onions become translucent.

Add the tomato and celery leaves and cook, stirring, until the mixture looks like a thick paste. Mix in the brewer's yeast and soy sauce and stir until smooth.

Add the water and herbs and simmer 15 minutes. Strain the broth, discarding the vegetables. Makes 3 cups of rich brown stock. Shake well before using.

To store, freeze in an ice-cube tray. Use a cube at a time instead of bouillon cubes, to start soups, gravies and sauces, or drink straight up as bouillon. Serves 4.

Less than 100 calories per serving

Greens and Grains (*Cream of Spinach and Buckwheat Soup*)

½ *cup buckwheat groats (kasha)*
1 *small egg*
¾ *cup chopped onion*
2 *tablespoons butter*
3 *cups vegetable broth*
¼ *pound spinach*
¼ *teaspoon nutmeg*
¼ *teaspoon ground ginger*
2 *cups milk or Vegetable Milk (see p. 64)*
pepper to taste
croutons

In a saucepan combine groats (kasha) and egg, lightly beaten. Cook the mixture over moderate heat until the grains separate.

In a small skillet sauté onion in butter for 3 minutes.

Combine the onion with the groats, add vegetable broth; spinach, washed and trimmed; and nutmeg and ground ginger. Cook the mixture, covered, over moderately low heat for 15 minutes, or until the groats are tender.

Transfer the mixture to a blender or to a food processor fitted with a steel blade and puree until smooth.

Pour the puree into a large saucepan, stir in milk, and add pepper to taste.

Heat the soup over moderate heat until hot, ladle into heated bowls, and serve with croutons. Serves 4.

Less than 200 calories per serving

Soupçon I (*Lettuce and Green Pea Soup*)

> *1 large head (about 8 cups) iceberg, romaine, or leaf*
> * lettuce, shredded*
> *1 10-ounce package frozen green peas*
> *1 green onion, diced*
> *½ cup vegetable broth*
> *1½ cups skim milk*
> *Salt-free Salt I, II, or III (see pp. 60–61)*
> *¼ teaspoon nutmeg*
> *dash pepper*
> *8 thin lemon slices*

In 4-quart kettle, combine shredded lettuce, peas, green onion, and broth. Bring to boiling over medium heat. Reduce heat and simmer, covered, 10 minutes, or just until lettuce is soft.

In electric blender container or food processor, place half of lettuce mixture and liquid; cover and blend at high speed 1 minute. Pour into bowl. Repeat with remaining lettuce mixture and liquid. Pour all lettuce mixture back into kettle.

Add milk, "salt," nutmeg, and pepper to mixture in kettle. Cook over medium heat, stirring, until well blended.

Serve soup hot; or refrigerate until well-chilled—several hours. Serve garnished with lemon slices. Makes 8 servings.

For a super soupçon, sprinkle with a little cheese, a tablespoon of brewer's yeast, and bake at 400° F. until brown and bubbly.

Less than 100 calories per serving

Soupçon II

A two-way soup *or* salad.

> *2 large cucumbers*
> *Salt-free Salt I, II, or III (see pp. 60–61)*
> *2 cups yogurt*
> *3 teaspoons fresh chopped dill*
> *2 green onions, chopped*
> *lettuce*

Pare, halve, seed, and dice cucumbers; sprinkle lightly with Salt-free Salt; drain in colander ½ hour.

Mix cucumber with yogurt, dill, green onions, and dash Salt-free Salt.

Serve in lettuce-lined bowls.

VARIATION: For soup, whirl in blender with 2 cups buttermilk; top with chopped mixed sprouts. Serve with nearly raw veggies.* Makes 4 servings.

Less than 100 calories per serving

Exploded Dumpling Soup

2 tablespoons sifted flour
½ cup milk
2 whole eggs
Salt-free Salt I, II, or III (see pp. 60–61) to taste
6 cups boiling meat-free consommé

Mix flour, milk, eggs, and salt in a bowl.

Pour through a colander into boiling consommé and continue boiling for 5 minutes. Garnish with sprouts and sprinkle with a tablespoon of wheat germ or bran. Makes 8 servings. Keeps for a week.

Less than 125 calories per serving

---

* Bring out the bright color in those raw, firm vegetables (like green beans, broccoli, asparagus, peas, or carrots) with this quick-blanch method: Drop vegetables into a large potful of boiling water for 10 to 20 seconds; drain vegetables quickly and plunge immediately into a bowl of ice water. Drain, pat dry. Serve these extra-crispy vegetables cold in salads, or reheat in a skillet with oil and seasonings.

Sunchoke Soup (Mock Cream of Potato)

> *2 pounds Jerusalem artichokes*
> *2 cups boiling water*
> *1 tablespoon butter*
> *1 tablespoon flour*
> *½ cup milk or Vegetable Milk (see p. 64)*
> *½ cup plain yogurt*
> *1 egg yolk*
> *½ cucumber, sliced paper thin*
> *Salt-free Salt I, II, or III (see pp. 60–61) and pepper to*
> *   taste*
> *½ teaspoon paprika*

Cook Jerusalem artichokes in boiling water 15 minutes or until a fork pierces them easily. Drain, reserving liquid.

Slip off the skins and puree artichokes in a blender with the liquid. Melt butter in a saucepan, add flour; cook 2 minutes, stirring. Whisk in the hot artichoke mixture and simmer until slightly thickened.

Blend milk and yogurt with egg yolk. Gradually add to the soup, stirring constantly.

Add sliced cucumber and Salt-free Salt and pepper to taste. Sprinkle with ½ teaspoon paprika. Serves 4 to 6.

HINT: Jerusalem artichokes withstand cold winters, pop up very early. You can dig them up even in cold weather to use raw in crunchy salads or in stir-fry dishes, instead of water chestnuts. If you don't have them in your garden, the supermarket will be selling them as "sunchokes." Keep a few out from the package and plant them for a crop of your own (they spread every year).

Less than 100 calories per serving

Carrot-Yogurt Soup

¼ cup butter
8 medium carrots, scraped and thinly sliced
3 medium onions, chopped
4 cups Broth (see p. 82)
1 cup plain yogurt
½ cup skim milk or Vegetable Milk (see p. 64)
¼ cup fresh chopped chives, or 2 tablespoons freeze-dried
*   chives*

Melt butter in a large frying pan. Sauté carrots and onions until onions are tender. Add broth, cover, and simmer 1 hour.

Puree mixture in blender. Transfer to a 2-quart saucepan.

Add yogurt and milk, stirring until smooth. Keep on low heat until ready to serve, but do not allow to boil.

Sprinkle with chives. Makes 7 cups.

Less than 125 calories per serving

Green Pepper Gazpacho

1 large bell pepper, roasted, peeled, chopped
1½ cups freshly squeezed grapefruit juice
2 tomatoes, peeled, seeded, and finely diced
1 small cucumber, peeled, seeded, and grated
2 celery stalks, finely chopped
2 tablespoons fresh chopped parsley
4 almonds, blanched

Puree all ingredients in electric blender or food processor.

Garnish with almonds. Serve cold in chilled bowls. Makes 2–3 servings.

Less than 100 calories per serving

Alfalfacado Soup I

2 cups avocado, chopped
2 cups tomatoes, chopped
¾ cup tofu, chopped
½ cup chopped onion
1 clove garlic
2 tablespoons fresh parsley
2 tablespoons olive oil
1 tablespoon tamari
1 tablespoon lemon juice
1 teaspoon brewer's yeast
2 cups alfalfa sprouts

Put all ingredients into a blender except 1 cup of the avocado and 1½ cups of the alfalfa sprouts.

Blend and pour the mixture into a bowl with the reserved avocado and sprouts. Mix and serve. Makes 6 servings.

Less than 200 calories per cup

Alfalfacado Soup II

1 cup tomatoes, chopped
½ cup orange, peeled and chopped
1 cup avocado, chopped
alfalfa sprouts or sunflower seeds

Blend tomatoes, orange, and avocado in blender or food processor until creamy.

Pour into serving bowls and garnish with alfalfa sprouts or sunflower seeds.

If this soup is going to sit and wait to be served, prevent discoloration by stirring in a dab of mayonnaise. Thin, if needed, with water. Makes 3 cups.

Less than 200 calories per cup

Carrot Consommé

1 cup lentil sprouts
1 cup carrot juice
handful parsley leaves
handful watercress leaves or radish sprouts
caraway seeds
wafers (optional)

Mix lentil sprouts into a pulpy consistency with a little water. Add carrot juice, parsley leaves and watercress leaves or radish sprouts.
Put into blender a little at a time and puree.
Serve hot or cold sprinkled with caraway seeds accompanied by thin wafers. Makes 2½ cups.

Less than 100 calories per cup

Mock Split Pea Soup

1 heaping teaspoon Broth Powder (see p. 63)
1 teaspoon brewer's yeast
1–2 cups boiling water
1 teaspoon oil
*Salt-free Salt I, II, or III (see pp. 60–61) * to taste*

Pour boiling water over broth powder and brewer's yeast. Add oil and salt. Stir and enjoy. Serves 2.
HINT: Try it as a good pick-me-up in a thermos.

Less than 50 calories per cup

---

* Miss *real* salt? French tarragon's a dead ringer for salt.

SALADS

By Bean Alone (Lentil Salad)

> ¾ pound dried red lentils
> water to cover
> 2 teaspoons Broth Powder (see p. 63)
> 1 cup chopped parsley
> 1 cup chopped onion
> 1 cup finely chopped red or green pepper
> vinegar and oil to taste
> lettuce

Wash lentils and place in saucepan with enough water to cover. Cook the lentils for 15 minutes, then drain them.

Refill saucepan with enough broth powder and water to cover lentils. Slowly simmer the lentils until tender, about 40 minutes.

Drain and chill the lentils. Before serving, mix in the parsley, onion, and pepper, then season with oil and vinegar. Serve over chilled crisp torn lettuce leaves. Makes 6 servings.

HINT: If lettuce is a little limp, place briefly in a pan of cold water with a few potato slices. Then drain and pat dry.

Less than 125 calories per serving

Alfalfacado

Instant salad in a shell.

> 1 large avocado
> 1 tablespoon mayonnaise
> alfalfa sprouts

Halve avocado. Take out meat and beat with fork into mash.

Mix mashed avocado with mayonnaise and spoon back into shell halves. Garnish with alfalfa sprouts.

Less than 200 calories per half shell

Swee' Pea

1 cup raw shelled peas
1 quart shredded romaine lettuce
1 tomato, diced
2 tablespoons diced red onion
½ cup diced celery
¼ teaspoon dill seed
2 tablespoons fresh lemon juice
¼ cup sesame oil

Combine ingredients in a bowl and mix lightly. Makes 6 servings.

HINT: Don't buy a fancy lettuce drier. An old cotton pillowcase makes a container for keeping greens crisp and dry.

Less than 100 calories per serving

20 Carrots Tabouli

2 cups water
1 cup dry bulgur or cracked wheat
1 cup shredded carrot
1 large tomato, chopped
1 bunch whole green onions, sliced
1–2 teaspoons Salt-free Salt I, II, or III (see pp. 60–61) or
    kelp
½ teaspoon black pepper
1 cup finely chopped parsley
½ cup fresh finely chopped mint
3 tablespoons freshly squeezed, strained lemon juice
¼ cup cold-pressed olive oil

In a large serving bowl, combine the water and bulgur. Allow to stand for 1 to 2 hours, or until all the water is absorbed and the grain is tender.

Add the carrots, tomato, and onions to the bulgur. Season with Salt-free Salt and pepper. Sprinkle the salad with parsley, mint, and lemon juice. Pour in the olive oil.

Toss lightly. Adjust seasoning to taste, good with soup and crackers. Makes 6 servings.

Less than 150 calories per serving

Rough Cuts

> ½ *cup small cauliflower flowerets*
> ½ *cup each, cut ¼ inch thick diagonally:*
>   *carrots*
>   *celery*
>   *red bell pepper*
>   *zucchini*
> 4 *tomatoes, quartered*
> ¼ *cup Alfalfacado (see p. 90)*
> ¼ *teaspoon dill weed*
> 1 *tablespoon chopped chives*
> *lettuce (see* NOTE)

Steam cauliflower, carrots, and celery until just tender, yet still crisp and crunchy.

Cool, then combine with remaining ingredients except chives and lettuce. Chill 1 hour.

Add chives and serve on lettuce. Flavor improves on standing and salad will keep well up to 5 days. Makes 4 servings.

NOTE: Which lettuce you ask? Here's what nature offers you in her four major types:

100 GRAMS, OR 1 SERVING	VIT. A (I.U.)	VIT. C (MG.)	CALCIUM (MG.)	IRON (MG.)
Butterhead lettuce	970	8	35	2.0
Romaine lettuce	1,900	18	68	1.4
Crisphead lettuce	330	6	20	0.5
Loose-leaf lettuce	1,900	18	68	1.4

They are nearly equal in other vitamins, minerals, protein and carbohydrates.

Less than 75 calories per serving

Great Gratings I (*Hot Carrot Slaw*)

> *1 pound carrots (or more if necessary to fill the pan)*
> *4 tablespoons butter or oil*
> *Salt-free Salt I, II, or III (see pp. 60–61) and pepper to*
>   *taste*

Shred enough carrots to fill an 8-inch cast-iron pan to the brim. Place the carrots in pan and cook over high heat. Turn them regularly with a spatula so that the carrots will dehydrate and begin to brown evenly. When some begin to blacken and the rest are cooked and well dried out, reduce heat and add butter, Salt-free Salt, and pepper. Toss gently with spatula to blend.

Serve in a heated dish. Garnish with sliced radish and caraway seed. Makes 4 servings.

Less than 100 calories per serving

Great Gratings II

> *4 cups shredded red cabbage*
> *2 cups julienned or chopped beets*
> *3 large green apples, coarsely shredded*
> *⅔ cup Dieter's Mayonnaise (see recipe below)*
> *1 teaspoon Dijon mustard*
> *1 teaspoon curry powder*
> *pepper to taste*
> *parsley*

In a large bowl, toss cabbage, beets, and apples.
Prepare Dieter's Mayonnaise.
Mix together mayonnaise, mustard, and curry. Toss with salad and pepper to taste. Chill and garnish with parsley when serving. Makes 8 servings.

Less than 150 calories per serving

DIETER'S MAYONNAISE:
>   1 tablespoon lemon juice
>   1 cup creamy cottage cheese
>   1 tablespoon water

Place all ingredients in blender and blend on a medium speed until smooth and creamy. Use as you would sour cream or mayonnaise. For pink mayonnaise, add beet juice. Makes 1 cup.

10 calories per tablespoon

Great Gratings III

>   2 cups potatoes, boiled
>   2 cups raw sliced mushrooms
>   2 cups fresh sliced cucumber
>   1½ cups Yogurt Dressing

Slice potatoes, mushrooms, and cucumber. Blend with delicious low-fat Yogurt Dressing.

HINT: For quick sliced mushrooms use your hard-cooked egg slicer.

YOGURT DRESSING:
>   ½ cup olive oil
>   ½ cup apple cider vinegar
>   1 tablespoon prepared mustard
>   1 tablespoon lemon juice
>   1 clove garlic, pressed
>   1 tablespoon soy sauce (optional)
>   ½ teaspoon dill weed
>   ½ cup plain low-fat yogurt

In a medium bowl mix all ingredients together until thoroughly blended. Makes 1½ cups, 4 servings.

Less than 50 calories per tablespoon

Root Cellar Salad

A cabbage-plus kraut.

> *Chinese, red, or green cabbage*
> *escarole or romaine lettuce*
> *wild greens, such as dandelion, sorrel, or mustard*
> *kale*
> *turnips*
> *celery or cabbage celery*
> *red bell pepper*
> *¼ horseradish root*
> *sea salt, vegesalt, or sesame salt*
> *1 teaspoon ground pickling spices, or ½ teaspoon fresh*
>   *ground cayenne (available at health food stores)*
> *olive oil*

Wash the vegetables; peel, grate, and shred them.

Place in a bowl or crock in layers. Salt each layer. Add pickling spices. Put a smaller bowl inside the crock containing the vegetables and put a weight on top to press out any liquid that rises.

Salad will be ready to eat in a day, a week, a month. Before eating, pour off liquid and add olive oil. Good mixed with shredded lettuce or stirred into hot steamed buckwheat or millet. Makes 8–10 servings.

HINT: Got some limp root vegetables to revive? Soak them in ice water for an hour. And to be sure they don't lose flavor, add a teaspoon of honey.

Less than 200 calories per serving

Vitaminment Salad

> *½ pound fresh young spinach leaves, well washed and
>   dried*

DRESSING:

> *1 cup yogurt*
> *1 tablespoon olive oil*
> *1 tablespoon lemon juice*
> *½ teaspoon honey*
> *1 clove garlic, pressed*
> *1 tablespoon fresh chopped mint*
> *½ teaspoon salt*
> *roasted sesame seeds*

Toss together all but last ingredient in large bowl and re-frigerate until chilled, 1 to 2 hours.

Sprinkle with roasted sesame seeds and serve. Makes 4 servings.

NOTE: Low on energy? You may be low on potassium and sodium, and spinach's got 'em both—190 milligrams sodium and 790 milligrams potassium in 3.5 ounces. That's richer than beef, fish, poultry, or milk.

Less than 100 calories per serving

Hearts of the West

> *3 large celery stalks*
> *4 large celery hearts*
> *3 bunches mustard greens **
> *½ cup safflower oil*
> *4 tablespoons apple cider vinegar*
> *Salt-free Salt I, II, or III (see pp. 60–61)*
> *dash of cayenne*

Dice celery hearts and shred the stalks. Combine with greens in large bowl.

---

* Why are mustard greens a must? What else gives you so little (23 calories per ½ cup) and so much? Protein 2.2 grams; fat .4 grams; calcium 138 mg.; phosphorus 32 mg.; iron 1.8 mg.; sodium 18 mg.; potassium 220 mg.; vitamin A 5,800 I.U.; thiamine .8 mg.; riboflavin .14 mg.; niacin .6 mg.; vitamin C.

Mix oil with vinegar, Salt-free Salt, and cayenne. Add to salad. Toss well. OPTIONAL: Add a few cubes of tofu for protein, color, and practically no calories.

Less than 100 calories per serving

DRESSINGS

Mock Mayo I

6 ounces tofu
2 tablespoons mild vinegar
1 teaspoon prepared Dijon-style mustard
½ teaspoon tamari sauce
1 tablespoon sunflower oil

Combine first four ingredients in blender container and begin blending at lowest speed. When tofu is creamy, blend on higher speed and slowly pour oil into mixture. Continue blending until thoroughly combined. Makes 1½ cups.

VARIATION: Mock Green Goddess? Add ½ an avocado or a handful of parsley, cress, or fresh dill.

Less than 11 calories per tablespoon

Mock Mayo II

1 cup low-fat cottage cheese
2 tablespoons oil
1 tablespoon water
1 tablespoon cider vinegar
1 teaspoon dry mustard
½ teaspoon paprika
dash pepper

Blend all ingredients together in blender until smooth, occasionally stopping to scrape sides with rubber spatula. Thin with extra water if necessary.

VARIATION: Russian dressing? Whip in 1 tablespoon of catsup and you've got it.

Less than 28 calories per tablespoon

Ultimato Salad Dressing

1 tablespoon chives
1 tablespoon onion powder
1 cup tomato juice
*2 tablespoons lemon juice or vinegar **
½ tablespoon celery seed
1 tablespoon garlic powder

Combine all ingredients in blender and mix thoroughly. Chill.

Shake well before serving. Good on any green. Excellent over sliced tomatoes or chilled, steamed snow peas.

Less than 50 calories per cup

High-C Salad Dressing

Herb-rich and salt-free.

2 fresh lemons
1 teaspoon fresh grated horseradish root, or 1 teaspoon
   bottled sauce
⅔ cup olive oil
fresh black pepper to taste

Peel the lemon and dry the peel for other uses. Chop remainder, seeds and all, and puree in blender.

Combine with horseradish and remaining ingredients. Toss with the greens of your choice. Makes 1 cup.

HINT: For a quick colorful dressing with bite (for mild-flavored greens), grate both fresh horseradish and red radishes into sour cream or plain yogurt.

The *Armoracia lapathifolia* (horseradish) is an age-old digestant, has more vitamin C than ordinary lettuce or green pepper, and is rich in a sinus-clearing mineral-rich oil, known as allyl isothiocyanate.

Less than 75 calories per tablespoon

---

* Better yet, make your own fragrant true blue vinegar. Add borage flower blossoms to a bottle of white vinegar.

Low-Calorie Thousand Island Dressing

½ cup mashed tofu
½ cup yogurt
pepper to taste
¼ cup salad oil, or less
½ teaspoon dry mustard
2 tablespoons tomato paste
1 tablespoon carrot juice or water
3 teaspoons chopped pickles or pickled carrots

Blend first 5 ingredients. Thin if necessary with more yogurt.

Stir tomato paste, carrot juice or water, and pickles into above mixture.

Store dressing in the refrigerator. Yields 2 cups. Use as a vegetable dip or a spoon-on dressing.

Less than 50 calories per tablespoon

Main Dishes, Side Dishes, Gravies and Sauces

MAIN DISHES

Ma Bell

8 medium-size pepper shells
2 cups cooked soybeans *
2 tablespoons chopped onion
1 tablespoon melted butter
1 cup chopped celery
1 cup chopped peppers
1 teaspoon Broth Powder (see p. 63)
½ cup tomato juice
½ teaspoon sage
1 cup fresh finely shredded carrots
paprika

Preheat oven to 400° F. Prepare peppers by removing seeds and covering shells with boiling water a moment; drain.

Mash soybeans and add other ingredients. Fill pepper shells with soybean stuffing and add a dash of paprika to each shell.

Place stuffed peppers in casserole with ½ inch of water. Cover and bake for 45 minutes. Remove the cover for the last 10 minutes to brown peppers. Serve with a gravy or sauce if desired. Makes 8 servings.

Less than 300 calories per serving

* To trim calories, substitute 1 cup soy, lentil, or garbanzo sprouts for 1 cup beans.

Vegetarian Stroganoff *(Mushroom-Tofu Stew)*

SAUCE:

> 8 ounces tofu
> ⅓ cup water
> 2 tablespoons soy sauce
> 2 tablespoons lemon juice or apple cider vinegar
> 1 clove garlic
> 1 teaspoon chopped lemon rind
> 1 teaspoon chopped ginger root

Combine all ingredients in blender container; blend until very smooth. Be sure garlic, lemon rind, and ginger root are finely chopped, not left in big chunks.

Set aside or refrigerate until ready to use. Flavor improves on standing. Sauce will keep up to one week.

STEW:

> ½ onion, minced
> 1 clove garlic, minced (optional)
> 1 teaspoon vegetable oil
> ¾ pound fresh mushrooms, sliced
> 4 ounces tofu, cut in 1-inch cubes
> 2 tablespoons yogurt
> ½ teaspoon oregano
> 1 tablespoon slivered almonds, toasted
> sprouts
> 1 tablespoon chopped parsley

Sauté onion and garlic in oil until onion is transparent. Add mushrooms and sauté until slightly limp and moisture has evaporated. Push aside and add tofu cubes to brown slightly.

Pour sauce over all. Mix well and heat through, stirring. Blend in yogurt and oregano. Serve over Perfect Brown Rice (see p. 120) and sprinkle with toasted almonds or sprouts and parsley. Makes 4 servings.

Less than 250 calories per serving with ¼ cup steamed rice

Mock Veal Chops

>   *1 cup chopped mushrooms*
>   *1 cup pureed peas*
>   *1 egg*
>   *1 medium onion, minced*
>   *1 potato, peeled, boiled and mashed*
>   *2 tablespoons minced parsley*

COATING:

>   *cornmeal or flour*
>   *paprika*

Combine everything but coating ingredients. Shape into cutlets.

Roll in cornmeal mixture.

Bake in a lightly greased skillet. Serve with Mock Mayonnaise I or II (see p. 97) or any tomato gravy. Makes 4 servings.

VARIATION: Shape, as with croquettes, and bake in a 350° oven, turning twice.

HINT: For onions without tears: You'll weep no more if you cut the root end of the onion off last; freeze or refrigerate onions before chopping them up; peel under cold running water; periodically rinse hands under cold water while chopping.

Less than 100 calories per serving

Sprout Soufflé

> *3 tablespoons butter*
> *1 tablespoon chopped shallots or scallions*
> *2½ tablespoons unbleached white flour or whole wheat*
>   *flour*
> *2 cups nonfat milk*
> *1 cup chopped sprouts*
> *dash of cayenne*
> *1 tablespoon lemon juice*
> *1 egg yolk*
> *1 tablespoon low-fat milk*
> *4 egg whites, beaten stiff*
> *1 tablespoon grated Parmesan cheese*

In heavy saucepan, melt butter and stir in shallots. Cook gently 2 to 3 minutes. Add flour and make a roux. Add nonfat milk and sprouts and stir until smooth and bubbly.

Add cayenne and lemon juice to taste. Cook about 10 minutes and pour into a bowl to cool. Preheat oven to 350° F.

Meanwhile, beat egg yolk and low-fat milk and stir into sprout mixture while it is still warm. Cool in a bowl over ice water.

When cold, whip egg whites until stiff and fold into sprout mixture. Sprinkle with cheese. Bake for 35 minutes. Makes 4 servings.

Leftovers? Cut into squares and save. For tomorrow's lunch, sauté in a lightly oiled skillet, or sprinkle with oil and paprika and reheat in a hot oven.

Less than 75 calories per serving

20 Carrots Loaf

> 2 tablespoons whole-wheat bread crumbs
> ¾ cup grated raw carrot, packed
> 1 small onion, minced
> 1 stalk celery with leaves, thinly sliced
> ½ cup chopped sunflower or pumpkin seeds
> 2 tablespoons chopped parsley
> 2 tablespoons cream
> 2 eggs, slightly beaten
> 1½ teaspoons Salt-free Salt I, II, or III (see pp. 60–61)
> buttered whole-wheat bread crumbs
> butter

Preheat oven to 350° F. In a bowl mix thoroughly all the ingredients except the buttered bread crumbs.

Butter a loaf pan well and cover the bottom thickly with the bread crumbs. Pack in the loaf mixture and dot the top with butter.

Cover and bake for 30 minutes. Uncover the last 5 minutes of baking.

Remove from the oven, loosen the sides by running a knife around, and invert over a platter. Turn out the loaf and serve with tomato sauce, Golden Gravy (see p. 124), and a handful of sprouts, and a spoonful of low-calorie mayonnaise. Serves 2–3.

Less than 150 calories per serving

Three-Bean Stew

> 1 pound mushrooms
> 4 tablespoons vegetable oil
> 2 cloves garlic, minced or pressed
> 3 carrots, sliced
> 3 stalks celery, cut into ½-inch pieces
> ¼ cup chopped parsley
> ½ teaspoon coarsely ground pepper

¼ *teaspoon basil*
½ *teaspoon marjoram*
½ *cup each garbanzo beans, black-eyed peas, and navy*
   beans, soaked overnight in 5 cups of water
1 *pound stewed tomatoes, in juice*
½ *cup water*
1 *large red onion, sliced*
1 *cup cooked rice*

Sauté the mushrooms in oil. Add garlic, carrots, celery, parsley, pepper, and herbs.

Add the beans. Then add the tomatoes with their juice, and the water.

Mix in the sliced onion. Bring to a boil, then cover the pot. Simmer for 20 to 25 minutes. Add rice. Quickly place the covered pot into a low oven. Cook an additional 45 minutes. Makes 8 servings.

Less than 200 calories per serving

• Don't ban the beans! Beans contain two nonabsorbable carbohydrates, raffinose and stachyose, which are readily fermented by bacteria that live in the colon. But all beans were *not* created equal in their gas-producing ability. Here is a guide to the best and the worst for legume lovers who would rather shop around than switch: soybeans (the most); pink beans; black beans; pinto beans; California small white beans; great northern beans; lima beans (baby); garbanzos; lima beans (large); and black-eyes (the least).

The volume of flatus has been shown to increase tenfold after a meal of beans. But cooking beans with an equal portion of rice will eliminate up to 65 percent of their flatulence and increase the amount of usable protein.

Quick Quiche

½ pound green beans
½ pound zucchini, sliced
6 carrots, diced
½ cup fresh chopped parsley
6 spring onions (white and green part)
6 stalks celery, diced
1 teaspoon Salt-free Salt I, II, or III (see pp. 60–61)
1 teaspoon pepper
2 eggs, beaten
¼ cup skim milk
¼ cup Ricotta cheese
1 ounce Parmesan cheese, grated
dash of nutmeg
1 tablespoon butter
oil

Steam each vegetable separately. Preheat oven to 400° F. Mix with all remaining ingredients except Parmesan cheese.

Place in a shallow baking dish that has been lightly oiled. Dust with grated Parmesan cheese (optional) and bake 10 to 15 minutes. Makes 6 servings.

Less than 275 calories per serving

Spaghetti with No-Cook Sauce

Here's a straight-from-the-garden fresh tomato sauce and spaghetti dish.

SAUCE:

> 2–3 ripe, juicy tomatoes
> 1 teaspoon fresh chopped basil, or ½ teaspoon dried leaf
>   basil
> 2 tablespoons chopped green onions
> dash of pepper
> ½ teaspoon honey

PASTA:

> ½ pound spaghetti
> 2 tablespoons olive oil
> handful raw shredded carrot
> grated Parmesan cheese (optional)

Peel, seed, and chop tomatoes (about 2 cups).
Mix well with basil, or green onions, pepper, and honey.
Cook spaghetti in salted water.

Toss drained, steaming hot spaghetti with olive oil and carrot, then add the tomato sauce and toss all together. Serve right away with breadsticks, grated Parmesan. Makes 4 cups.

NOTE: Instead of high-calorie, high-sodium Parmesan, try frozen, slightly thawed and shredded tofu. Or soak in soy sauce before freezing.

Less than 100 calories per ¼ cup

Shoestring Stew

> 2 onions
> 2 parsnips
> 2 carrots
> 5 cups water
> 1 cup millet
> 1 tablespoon vegetable oil
> 1 cup chopped mushrooms
> 1 cup firm julienned tofu
> 1 bay leaf
> 1 pinch thyme or basil
> 2 tablespoons soy sauce

Cut onions into 6 or 8 wedges; cut carrots and parsnips into shoestrings.

Bring water to a boil in large pot. Place frying pan on medium heat, add millet, and stir constantly until color changes slightly and a nutlike fragrance is given off. Add millet to boiling water, reduce heat to simmer, and cover.

Return frying pan to medium heat and add oil. When oil is hot add onions. Stir for a few minutes, then add carrots, and parsnips. Stir a few more minutes and add mushrooms and tofu; stir again.

Add vegetables and herbs to millet and simmer, covered, for 30 to 40 minutes or until vegetables are tender.

Stir once or twice while cooking and add soy sauce about 5 minutes before end. Makes 6 servings.

NOTE: Millet is high in calcium and B vitamins, lower in calories than rice (100 per ½ cup), and a cinch to digest.

Less than 150 calories per serving

Fungus-Among-Us Cutlets *(Cheese and Mushroom Chops)*

1 cup finely chopped mushrooms
1 green onion, minced
2 eggs
½ cup bread or cracker crumbs
½ cup grated mild Cheddar
butter

Mix all ingredients well, but do not turn into a mush. Pinch off about a teaspoon of mix and sauté in a little butter until done. Taste and adjust seasoning if necessary. Form mix into 8 patties about ¾ inch thick and press into shape between sheets of waxed paper. Chill.

Sauté patties in butter over low heat. The outside of the cutlet should be crisp and the inside should be moist. Serve plain, or add additional grated cheese before serving. Delicious with any sauce. Makes 4 servings. Well wrapped, it freezes for future lunches and suppers. Try the recipe below for a good side dish.

Less than 100 calories per plain serving

CARAMEL CARROTS:
3 medium carrots, scraped and sliced
3 small knobs celery root or heart, sliced
1 tablespoon sesame oil

Preheat heavy clay pot or Dutch oven to 425° F. Put in carrots, celery root or heart, and sesame oil.

Cover and roast for 60 minutes until vegetables caramelize and make their own good gooey gravy. Makes 2 servings.

Less than 75 calories per serving

Mung Foo Yung

4 eggs, beaten
1 cup mung bean sprouts
6 green onions (including tops), sliced
½ cup shredded celery
oil

SAUCE:

2 tablespoons arrowroot
1 cup water
soy sauce to taste

Combine ingredients and cook like pancakes in a heavy, lightly oiled pan.

Make sauce by blending ingredients in a saucepan and cooking until thickened. Serve over patties. Makes 6 servings.

Less than 150 calories per serving

HINT: If you'd like to raise your own sprouts, here's how: Place about 1 inch of mung beans in the bottom of a quart jar. Cover beans with water and soak overnight. Place a square of nylon net over top of jar and secure with a jar ring. The next morning, pour off water and lay jar on its side, keeping nylon net in place. Rinse 2 or 3 times daily. Sprouts should be ready to eat in a few days.

Mung beans, when sprouted, contain an auxin or plant hormone that can actually reverse the aging process and make cells younger. Burned-out racehorses have been brought back to record-breaking running power after being fed on these sprouts.

Mock Salmon Loaf

2 cups finely grated carrots
1 cup shredded celery
¼ cup ground sunflower seeds
1 tablespoon low-calorie mayonnaise or yogurt
2 tablespoons peanut butter
1 teaspoon Salt-free Salt I, II, or III (see pp. 60–61)
1 teaspoon good paprika

Mix all ingredients in a large bowl. Mold into loaf and serve with garnish.

Use as a spread or stuff raw celery or tomato halves. You can also make mock salmon sandwiches on low-calorie bread, wrap well, and freeze individually for future emergency bag lunches. (They'll defrost by lunchtime.)

NOTE: If you grow your own red peppers you can make your own paprika. Toss dried pods (a blend of banana and sweet bell peppers is best) into blender, and buzz until powdered. For coarse herbs, stop blender before contents are powdery. Pour through strainer and reserve. Bottle up the powder and use the rest for flavoring gravies, stews, soups.

Less than 100 calories per ¼ cup

Plain Green Wrappers

The crepe alternative.

> *6 large Boston lettuce leaves, well rinsed and patted dry*
> *¼ cup fresh, loosely packed coriander leaves (also called*
>   *Chinese parsley, cilantro, and culantro; available in*
>   *Chinese and Spanish markets)*
> *½ cup fresh, loosely packed mint leaves*
> *¼ cup chopped scallion*
> *1 cup Perfect Brown Rice (see p. 120), hot or cold*
> *Avocado Sauce (p. 121), Golden Gravy (p. 124), or any*
>   *Mock Mayo (p. 97)*

Open a lettuce leaf and add a sprig of Chinese parsley, one or two mint leaves, chopped scallion, and a spoonful of rice.

Wrap the leaf around. Using the fingers, dip the "package" into sauce and eat with your fingers. Makes 6.

Less than 100 calories per rolled leaf

Plain Brown Wrappers

The ultimate soy-flour crepe.

> *2 eggs*
> *2 tablespoons orange juice*
> *4 tablespoons soy powder*
> *1 teaspoon arrowroot*
> *1 teaspoon sesame seeds*

In a bowl, beat ingredients until smooth. Cover and re-frigerate for at least 1 hour to improve consistency.

Grease a heavy iron skillet liberally. Heat until very hot.

Spoon in 1 tablespoon of batter, tipping to coat pan. Cook until dry. Loosen edges, turn, cook 1 minute. Repeat until batter is finished.

Spread with any sugar-free jelly or pureed tofu. Roll and eat out of hand or dribble with Decalorized Honey (see recipe below). Makes 6 big crepes.

Less than 100 calories per plain crepe

DECALORIZED HONEY:
> *¼ cup warm water*
> *¼ cup honey*
> *1 tablespoon fruit juice concentrate*

Combine water, honey, and juice concentrate. Heat gently and dribble over crepes.

Broiler-Maker Bean Curd

> *4 slices bean curd (about ½" x 4" x 4")*
> *soy sauce, preferably low sodium*
> *parsley*

SAUCE:
> *3 tablespoons minced onion*
> *5 tablespoons orange juice*
> *1 teaspoon grated orange peel*

1 tablespoon lemon juice
¼ teaspoon cinnamon powder
¼ cup red wine
1 teaspoon cornstarch or arrowroot mixed with 2
*   teaspoons water*

Preheat broiler. Brush the bean curd slices generously with soy sauce. Place on an oiled rack and broil, turning to brown both sides, brushing with soy sauce. Set aside. Keep warm.

Mix the first 6 sauce ingredients and bring to a boil.

Stir the cornstarch or arrowroot mixture into the boiling liquid. Pour over the bean curd. Serve hot over raw spinach, dandelion greens, or shredded Chinese cabbage. Sprinkle with chopped parsley. Makes 4 servings.

Less than 75 calories per serving

Green Pea Soufflé

2 cups cooked green peas
2 eggs, separated
⅔ cup sweet cream, or ⅓ cup cream plus ⅓ cup yogurt
1 teaspoon Salt-free Salt I, II, or III (see pp. 60–61)

Preheat oven to 350° F. Combine in bowl green peas, egg yolks, cream, yogurt, and "salt."

Fold in stiffly beaten egg whites. Spoon into greased casserole dish and bake 30 minutes. Makes 4 servings.

VARIATION: Substitute 2 cups steamed asparagus for green peas.

NOTE: Peas are a superstar source of B_3 (niacin), which aids in carbohydrate and protein metabolism, releasing energy in food. Helps maintain healthy skin and helps to relieve mental disturbances by correcting certain enzyme deficiencies. Recommended adult daily minimum: 12 to 20 milligrams. Peas have twice the B_3 of lima beans or asparagus.

Less than 150 calories per serving

Vegetarian Steak Tartar

> 1 medium eggplant, or 2 small ones
> salt
> ¼ cup butter or vegetable oil
> 1½ cups milk, or Vegetable Milk (see p. 64)
> 2 eggs, lightly beaten
> 1 cup crushed low-calorie whole-wheat wafers
> pinch of pepper
> cinnamon
> lemon juice
> Tabasco sauce
> sesame seeds
> paprika
> alfalfa sprouts

Preheat oven to 350° F. Peel, slice, and cook eggplant in salted water until very tender. Or bake unpeeled eggplant until it is soft, then peel and slice.

Mash eggplant with butter or oil while still warm. Add milk, eggs, and wafer crumbs; season.

Wet your hands. Shape mixture into patties. Arrange on greased cookie sheets. Bake for 10 minutes. Turn and bake until dry to the touch. Sprinkle with sesame seeds. Good with sautéed tofu cubes.

Serve with Green Gravy I or II (pp. 121–122) or cover with Golden Gravy (p. 124), sprinkle with paprika, and return to oven and bake at 400° F. until brown and bubbly. Garnish with sprouted alfalfa. Makes 4–5 servings.

Less than 200 calories per serving

SIDE DISHES

Parsleyed Cucumbers

> 4 medium-size (½ pound each) cucumbers
> Salt-free Salt to taste I, II, or III (see pp. 60–61), or kelp
> 2 tablespoons butter

pepper to taste
finely chopped parsley for garnish

Trim off and discard the ends of the cucumbers. Cut cucumber in half widthwise, then quarters lengthwise. Using a paring knife, pare away the skin and cut away most of the center seeds, but leave some of the soft center pulp.

Drop the cucumber pieces into boiling salted water and cook about 5 minutes. Drain and run under cold running water until chilled. Drain well.

Heat the butter in a skillet and add the cucumbers. Add salt and pepper to taste. Toss until thoroughly heated and serve sprinkled with chopped parsley. Makes 8 servings.

VARIATION: A more sensual substitute for parsley? Try fresh coriander or Chinese parsley, also sold as cilantro at Italian, Spanish, and Oriental greengrocers.

Less than 50 calories per serving

20 Carrots Tofu

1 cup mashed tofu
¼ cup milk or yogurt
1 egg
¼ cup Parmesan cheese
pepper or Pepper Plus (see p. 62) to taste
dash nutmeg
5 large carrots, sliced and cooked until tender
1 small onion, thinly sliced
½ cup cashew nuts
butter

Preheat oven to 350° F. Blend first 6 ingredients in blender jar.

Arrange the carrots and sliced onions in a greased 1½-quart casserole. Pour the tofu mixture over the carrots and onions.

Top with cashews and dot with butter. Bake for 45 minutes. Makes 6 servings.

Less than 150 calories per serving

Sprouted Spaetzle (Noodle Dumplings)

> 1 egg
> 1 cup whole grain flour
> ½ cup chopped sprouts
> 3 quarts water
> 1 tablespoon salt

Break egg into a bowl. Add flour and sprouts, stirring to make a smooth dough. Add water to make a heavy batter.

Bring to a boil salted water in a pot. Dip a small cutting board into the boiling water. Place about ⅓ of the batter on the board and cut strips of the batter off the edge of the board, letting the knife enter the boiling water each time you make a cut. The spaetzle are cooked when they float.

Remove the dumplings with a skimmer. Store in a warm bowl. Continue cutting the spaetzle until all the batter is used. Makes 2 to 3 servings. Serve on picks and dip in a saucer of plain yogurt laced with lots of crushed chopped garlic and minced scallion. Cut up and add to salads. Or serve with One Tomato, Two Tomato Gravy (p. 122), Avocado Sauce (p. 121), or Low-Calorie Pesto (p. 123).

Less than 150 calories per plain serving

Carrot Kugelhupf

> 2½ cups thinly sliced carrots
> 4 tablespoons water
> 2-4 tablespoons butter
> ½ cup Broth (p. 82)
> pepper or Pepper Plus (see p. 62)
> 10 tablespoons diced mushrooms
> 1 shallot or green onion, minced
> 2 eggs
> 2¼ tablespoons grated Swiss cheese
> 1 tablespoon chervil or parsley

In a large pot cook carrots, water, 2 tablespoons butter, broth, and pepper to taste. Puree. Preheat oven to 200°–220° F.

Sauté mushrooms with 1 tablespoon butter in a pan with the shallot. Mix mushrooms into the carrot puree.

In a bowl, mix eggs, cheese, chervil or parsley, and combine with carrot puree.

Line the interior of a medium-size, glazed terra-cotta mold (for kugelhupf) with a thin film of butter. Pour in the carrot mixture and set the mold in a pan of water. Cook in oven for about 45 minutes. Makes 4 servings.

Less than 100 calories per serving

O. J. Carrots

> 1 pound carrots, scraped, sliced, and steamed * until
>   barely tender
> 1 cup Broth (see p. 82)
> 1 orange, juice and grated rind
> 1 tablespoon orange juice concentrate
> butter to taste
> 2 tablespoons cornstarch or arrowroot
> ¼ cup cold water

After carrots are cooked, reserve, and measure 1 cup broth for sauce. Add grated rind and juice of orange, the orange juice concentrate, and butter. Bring to a boil.

Add the starch, which has been mixed with cold water (to prevent lumping) to the sauce. Stir until smooth and thick. Pour over carrots. Makes 4 servings.

HINT: A good "mini-dinner" or brunch. Just add crackers and tea. Leftovers? Puree, and reheat to use as a meatloaf "gravy."

Less than 100 calories per serving

---

* Boiling leaks out half to three-quarters of a vegetable's essentials. And in the case of carrots, the two nutrients of which you'll lose the most are calcium and potassium—the ones carrots especially contain.

Parsley Home Fries

12 large, fresh, crisp parsley sprigs
vegetable oil for frying

Wash and dry parsley thoroughly.

Heat vegetable oil in pan to 380° F. Drop sprigs in by the handful and lift out almost immediately with a slotted skimmer. Drain on paper towels. Eat while hot.

Less than 25 calories a sprig

Green Pepper Home Fries

4 medium green peppers, quartered
1 quart plus 2 teaspoons water
salt
1½ cups walnuts, pecans, or almonds
2 eggs
vegetable oil for frying

Cut pepper into matchsticks. Cover with 1 quart boiling salted water and allow to stand for 20 minutes.

Finely chop, crush, or grate nuts. Beat eggs together with 2 teaspoons water. Heat enough oil in a heavy skillet to deep-fry.

Drain pepper sticks well and pat dry. Dip first in beaten egg, then in nuts. Fry quickly to a crisp golden brown. Drain briefly on paper towel before serving. Eat while warm.

VARIATION: Dip in fresh pureed tofu or yogurt with plenty of fresh mashed garlic, or simply squirt with ginger juice.

Less than 50 calories per 2-quarter serving

Tofu "Bacon"

1 block fresh firm tofu
½ cup regular or low-sodium soy sauce
1 teaspoon hickory-flavored seasoning or Salt-free
  Seasoning Paste (see p. 61)

sesame oil
turmeric
sesame or poppy seeds

Cut tofu into ½-inch slices then 1-inch strips. (Thawed frozen tofu may also be used.)

Marinate 2 or more hours in soy sauce with hickory-flavored seasoning or Salt-free Seasoning Paste.

Drain and brush once with sesame oil and sprinkle with turmeric. Broil 5 to 8 minutes on each side. Sprinkle with sesame or poppy seeds. Serve with steamed rice and a platter of raw vegetables.

Less than 150 calories per serving

Radishes in Mustard Sauce

1 pound radishes

SAUCE:

½ cup vegetable oil
3 tablespoons white wine
¼ teaspoon dry mustard
¼ teaspoon Salt-free Salt I, II, or III (see pp. 60–61)
¼ teaspoon pepper or Pepper Plus (see p. 62)
1 teaspoon parsley flakes
1 teaspoon lemon juice

Thinly slice radishes and place in covered baking dish. Preheat oven to 350° F.

Beat all sauce ingredients vigorously until well blended.

Pour sauce over radishes. Bake, covered, for 30 minutes until radishes are pink and soft. Makes 4 servings.

NOTE: Radishes are not only virtually calorie-free, they come in three colors (red, white, and black), all of which are rich in vitamin C and other infection-fighting nutrients. Besides baking them, you can even broil or fry them as a substitute for cherry tomatoes. Try radishes in Golden Gravy (p. 124).

Less than 150 calories per serving

Perfect Brown Rice

> *1½ cups brown rice*
> *1 egg*
> *3½ cups water or vegetable broth*
> *1 tablespoon vegetable oil or butter*

Preheat oven to 350° F. Combine rice and egg; sauté over moderate heat in a deep saucepan (1½ quart) until kernels are dry and separate. Add water or broth, and oil or butter.

Bring to a boil. Cover and place in oven for 45 minutes. Fluff when finished. Leftovers may be frozen in plastic tubs. Just steam to reheat.

To serve as a meal or snack, spoon into plastic bags in ½-cup servings. Put smaller bags in one large sack. Freeze. To reheat, steam 10 minutes and eat. Makes 6 servings.

VARIATIONS: Perfect Brown Rice Plus? Spoon a mouthful of rice onto a fresh leaf of Boston lettuce. Roll up, and munch like a mock crepe. Or dip in a bit of spicy mustard thinned with skim milk. Pluperfect Brown Rice? Substitute ½ cup lightly toasted raw millet, triticale whole rye kernels, or whole wheat for ½ cup rice.

Less than 150 calories per serving

Carrot Top Condiment

Nice with rice.

> *1 bunch young carrots with tops*
> *1 tablespoon sesame oil*
> *2 tablespoons tamari soy sauce*

Puree the carrots, with tops and stalks, in a food processor.

Heat the oil in a heavy frying pan. Sauté the puree until it begins to dry (2 to 3 minutes). Stir in soy sauce and remove from heat. Use as a side dish or vegetable dip. Makes about 4 cups.

Less than 100 calories per tablespoon

GRAVIES AND SAUCES

Avocado Sauce

2 avocados, peeled
1 tablespoon lemon juice
2 tablespoons grated onion
1 canned green chili
*3 tablespoons enchilada sauce, or 1½ tablespoons tomato
    paste*
¼ teaspoon brewer's yeast

Put all ingredients in blender and puree.

Cover well, refrigerate until serving time. Serve as "sauce on the side" with any hot or cold meatless main dish. Also good as a dip or spread. Makes about 2½ cups.

Less than 100 calories per tablespoon

Green Gravy I

½ zucchini
1 small avocado
3 celery stalks
1 seeded, chopped whole sweet bell pepper
½ hot bell pepper
2 shallots
curry powder to taste
3 tablespoons sunflower seeds

Blend ingredients in a food processor or blender. Also good as a cold dip or cold gravy. Or, heat gently and serve over meatless loaves and steamed veggies.

Less than 100 calories per ¼ cup

Green Gravy II

1 avocado
3 celery stalks
2 tablespoons raw sesame seed or peanut butter
1 tablespoon roasted pepper or pimento
1 small scallion
3 small garlic cloves, peeled
dash of cayenne pepper
½ cup tiny new potatoes, steamed and halved, or lentil
sprouts

Puree all ingredients except potatoes or sprouts in blender or food processor. Mix in potatoes or sprouts by hand.

Good cold or hot as a gravy or a dip. Yield: 2 cups.

Less than 100 calories per ¼ cup

One Tomato, Two Tomato Gravy

2 cups fresh chopped tomatoes
5 tablespoons unsalted butter
freshly ground pepper
wine, water, or juice

Place tomatoes in uncovered saucepan or skillet and, stirring frequently, heat to gentle bubbling. Keep heating, stirring regularly, until tomatoes form a thick puree and volume has been reduced to about ½ cup, in about 40 minutes. The puree does not have to be absolutely smooth.

Blend 5 tablespoons butter into puree, mixing thoroughly. Season with pepper to taste. Place in a storage jar and refrigerate until cooled.

Dilute with a little wine, water, or juice to use as a sauce. May also be used as a butter undiluted. Or add a tablespoon of yogurt or mashed tofu and use as a dip.

Less than 100 calories per tablespoon as a butter;
50 calories per tablespoon as a sauce

Low-Calorie Pesto

5 medium cloves garlic
1½–2 cups fresh, washed basil leaves, drained dry
½ cup frozen half-thawed, finely shredded tofu
¼ cup medium–coarsely chopped pine nuts **
¼ cup freshly grated Parmesan cheese
½ cup olive oil
freshly ground black pepper to taste

Crush the garlic and basil in a mortar and work them into a paste. (This can be done in the food processor or blender, but the texture of the finished sauce is much better if it's done by hand.)

Using fine cheesecloth, add tofu and squeeze the excess moisture out of the paste. Transfer the paste back to the mortar and mix in the pine nuts and cheese, working the ingredients well with the pestle to mix thoroughly.

Add olive oil a little at a time, stirring well after each addition, until all of it is incorporated. Adjust seasoning.

Just before the sauce is served, add about ¼ cup of boiling water and mix it in well. If serving with pasta, take the water from the cooking pot before the pasta is drained. This both heats the sauce and melts the cheese, allowing the flavors to blend. Makes 1 cup.

Less than 75 calories per tablespoon

* You may substitute oven-roasted sprouted chick-peas, finely crushed.

Golden Gravy

½ *cup brewer's yeast*
¼ *cup whole-grain flour*
⅓ *cup vegetable oil*
2–3 tablespoons soy sauce
¼ *teaspoon Pepper Plus (see p. 62) or fresh cracked black
    peppercorns*
water or vegetable broth, as needed

Toast the yeast and flour in a heavy skillet, stirring. Add the oil and stir with a whisk while it bubbles and turns golden brown. Add soy sauce and pepper. Stir.

Pour in water or broth, still stirring, until mixture thickens. Correct seasoning, if needed.

This recipe makes a good low-fat, low-sodium substitute for cheese sauce, or a good low-calorie fondue.

VARIATIONS: Stir in sautéed onions or mushrooms, chopped tomatoes, steamed peppers.

Less than 100 calories per ¼ cup

Beverages

Caffeine-free Coffees

CORN COFFEE:
Roast kernels of whole corn in the oven at 200° F. until brown all the way through. Put through coffee grinder or crush in food grinder. Boil or perk to desired strength. Or, roast coarse cornmeal the same way in a thin layer on a cookie sheet. Stir frequently until meal looks like ground coffee. Use about one tablespoon per cup.

SUNFLOWER COFFEE:
If you eat sunflower seeds in the shell, save those shells to make mocha java. Brown them, pour boiling water over them, cover, and let steep. Use one tablespoon per cup.

"INSTANT" COFFEE:
Oven-toast a slice of bread dark brown. Put it in a small saucepan. Pour a cup of boiling water over it. Cover, and let simmer for 1 minute. Press the liquid out of the toast with the back of a spoon. Enjoy a hearty mahogany cup of "near coffee."
HINT: The darker the toast, the darker the brew.

Less than 50 calories per plain cup of any Caffeine-free Coffee

Papaya Instant Breakfast

2 cups mashed ripe papaya
1 cup yogurt
2 tablespoons honey
½ teaspoon cinnamon

Blend ingredients in blender until smooth. This beverage is very easy on the stomach. Makes 2 servings.

Less than 150 calories per serving

Liquid Danish Pastry I

1 medium-size peach
¾ cup plain yogurt
½ teaspoon cinnamon
pinch nutmeg
pinch allspice
1–2 tablespoons honey
1 teaspoon grated orange rind

Peel peach and slice into blender jar; puree.

Add yogurt, cinnamon, nutmeg, and allspice. Whirl, then blend honey to taste.

Garnish with grated orange peel. Makes 1 cup.

Liquid Danish Pastry II

½ cup fresh blueberries
¾ cup plain yogurt
1 teaspoon lemon tea leaves, or 1 teaspoon grated lemon
*   rind*
¼ teaspoon ginger
1 teaspoon honey (optional)

Put fresh blueberries in blender jar and puree; then press through a wire strainer.

Return to blender, add yogurt, lemon tea leaves or grated lemon peel, plus ginger. Puree. Sweeten with honey. Makes 1 cup.

TIP: One cup of blueberries is only 93 calories and gives you 22.5 mg. calcium and 150 I.U. of vitamin A. And blueberries are rich in manganese, which aids the many other minerals and vitamins, especially B_1. And unlike most other berries, they seldom cause an allergic reaction.

Less than 200 calories per cup

Tiger's Milk

> *1 cup carrot juice*
> *3 cups fresh skim milk*
> *1-2 teaspoons vanilla extract*
> *1-3 teaspoons safflower oil*
> *½ cup noninstant powdered skim milk*
> *¼-½ cup brewer's yeast*

In blender jar pour carrot juice, 1 cup skim milk, vanilla extract, and safflower oil; blend for 1 minute.

Without stopping motor, add powdered skim milk and brewer's yeast.

Pour into pitcher and add 2 cups fresh skim milk. Refrigerate. Makes about 5 cups.

Less than 200 calories per ½ cup

Herbal Slim

> *1 tablespoon brewer's yeast*
> *1 quart tomato juice*
> *½ teaspoon vegetable salt*
> *1 tablespoon lemon juice*
> *1 tablespoon chopped parsley*
> *1 tablespoon chopped chives*
> *1 tablespoon chopped green onion*
> *1 teaspoon caraway seeds*

Blend all ingredients in blender. Makes 4 cups.

Less than 100 calories per cup

Hawaiian H$_2$O (*Coconut Cream and Coconut Juice*)

Using a hammer over a sink, crack 1 small coconut at four or five points. This should produce four or five large pieces. Discard inner coconut liquid.

Rest 1 piece at a time, shell side down, over a gas or electric burner. Let stand over moderately low heat for about 1 minute. Using a towel to protect your fingers, take the coconut and lift the fleshy part from the shell. It should come off easily. Using a swivel-blade vegetable scraper, scrape away the dark exterior, leaving only the white meat. Cut the meat into small cubes. There should be about 3 cups of cubes.

Add these cubes to the container of a food processor or electric blender. Add 2 cups of hot tap water. Blend until coconut meat is finely pulverized. Pour the liquid through a sieve into a bowl. Press and squeeze to extract excess liquid—about 5 cups. This is your "H$_2$O." Reserve the grated coconut. There should be about 2 cups of squeezed-out pulp. This is coconut cream. (If you add more water to the pulp and squeeze a second time, you will have a thinner liquid.)

Less than 300 calories per cup

Liquid Fruit Salad

> *1 large melon slice, cut into chunks*
> *½ cup cottage cheese, yogurt, or skim or Vegetable Milk*
>   *(p. 64)*
> *pinch of mint tea, mint extract, or spearmint leaves, or ½*
>   *teaspoon cinnamon **
> *½–1 cup water*

Mix in blender. Makes about 2 cups.

Less than 250 calories per cup

---

* Read 'em and weep. The cinnamon tree has one short sweet life. When the inner bark is harvested by a carved sickle to produce the characteristic roll of stick cinnamon, it dies.

Reducer Juicers

PINEAPPLE-CUCUMBER JUICE:

⅓ cucumber, peeled
1 ounce fresh pineapple
2 sprigs parsley
½ fresh apple, chopped
3 ice cubes

Combine and liquefy in blender. Makes 1 cup.

CARROT-APPLE JUICE:

2 ounces fresh apple juice
2 ounces fresh carrot juice
1 small apple, chopped
3 ice cubes

Combine and liquefy in blender. Makes 1 cup.
VARIATION: Two ounces of Hawaiian H_2O (see p. 128) may be used in place of either juice or coconut flakes pureed with water.

Less than 100 calories per cup

Sparkle Plenty Fruit Punch

2 cups apple juice
2 cups cherry juice
juice of 2 oranges
orange and lemon slices
1 pint carbonated mineral water

Combine juices and fruit slices in a punch bowl. Cover and marinate a few hours.

Just before serving, add mineral water and cracked ice.

Less than 250 calories per cup

Zero-Calorie Spritzer

Wipe a slice of lime around the inside of a stemmed wineglass. Drop in lime slice, add 2 ice cubes, and fill glass with chilled club soda. Makes 1 serving.

Russian Pop Rocks

2 pomegranates
2 cups cherries, raspberries, or strawberries
pinch of salt
sparkling mineral water

Juice pomegranates on a lemon reamer and set aside.

Place cherries, raspberries, or strawberries in a blender with a pinch of salt. Puree until smooth.

Put pureed berries through a sieve, extracting as much juice as possible. Combine berry and pomegranate juices, and add an equal amount of sparkling mineral water.

Pour into ice-cube trays; freeze. Serve "rocks" in iced herb tea, pink lemonade, or summer punches.

VARIATION: For Pop Rock Popsicles, pour juices into paper cups and, when partially frozen, insert sucker sticks. Freeze till solid. To eat, tear off paper cup and invert.

If you have a craving for strawberries, you may be vitamin-M deficient. Also known as folic acid, this nutrient is richly supplied by soybeans, lettuce, and mushrooms too.

Less than 250 calories in 8-ounce pop

Breads, Cereals, and Desserts

BREADS

Mock Pumpernickel

> 5 cups vegetable puree *
> 3 cups stone-ground whole-wheat flour
> 3 cups rye flour
> 4 tablespoons fresh minced dill
> 1 teaspoon salt

Combine puree, flour, and rye in a large mixing bowl. Mix thoroughly. If the mixture is too liquid to knead add more flour. If too dry add more liquid. Preheat oven to 375° F.

Knead the mixture for 10 minutes. Turn into an 8½″ × 4½″ × 2½″ breadpan.

Bake for 1 hour and 15 minutes.

Turn out onto a rack and cool. Bread has the consistency of a dense German pumpernickel and is delicious with very cold curls of butter (use a vegetable peeler) and curls of ice-cold carrots. Makes 1 loaf.

Less than 100 calories per slice

Cumberbuns

> 6 tablespoons butter
> 1 teaspoon grated orange rind
> 1 egg
> ⅔ cup honey
> 2 cups pastry flour
> 2 teaspoons baking powder
> ½ teaspoon ground nutmeg
> ½ teaspoon ground coriander

* Puree leftover cooked vegetables such as broccoli, kale, spinach, carrots, celery, celery root, or squash in a food processor with vegetable stock or water.

½ cup chopped nuts
½ cup currants or raisins
½ cup yogurt or Vegetable Milk (see p. 64)
½ cup fresh chopped parsley
⅔ cup grated cucumber

Preheat oven to 375° F. In a small bowl, beat 3 table-spoons butter, orange peel, egg, and honey.

Stir together the flour, baking powder, nutmeg, and coriander. Add nuts, raisins, and remaining butter, and stir alternately with milk, parsley, and cucumber into butter-egg mixture.

Combine well. Spoon into greased medium-size muffin cups, filling each about ⅔ full. Bake until muffins are golden and tops spring back when touched, 20 to 25 minutes. Remove from pan. Serve warm. Makes 12.

VARIATION: What else can you do with a muffin besides eat it? You can dip it in melted butter and ground pumpkin-pie spices.

Less than 175 calories per muffin

Breadless Breakfast Squares *(Tofu Toast)*

1 pound frozen tofu, thawed, rinsed, squeeze-dried,* and
*   cut into ½" squares*
seasoning to taste
2–3 tablespoons butter

Toast seasoned tofu cubes in a broiler or a toaster oven on a lightly oiled baking sheet until dry and crunchy. Turn as needed.

After the tofu has toasted, melt butter, pour over. Return squares to the oven and bake at 350° F. for an additional 10 to 15 minutes. Makes 8 squares.

* Simply freeze your store-bought tofu (soybean curd). Thaw at room temperature or in a low–warm oven and squeeze dry as you would a sponge.

VARIATION: Sprinkle hot toasted tofu squares with 1½ teaspoons finely grated cheese or try Breakfast Jam (below).

Less than 75 calories per square

BREAKFAST JAM:

In a blender, puree a quantity of one of the following fresh fruits: chopped apples, peaches, pears, or other fruit, and an almost equal weight of pitted dates.

Less than 50 calories per mouthful

Hair Breadths

Hardly a calorie in a whole mouthful but ten times as nutritious as conventional crackers.

> ¼ *cup whole-wheat or rye berries (sold at any health food store)*
> *Salt-free Salt I, II, or III (see pp. 60–61) to taste*

TOMATO JAM:

> *1 ripe firm tomato*
> *2 fresh basil leaves, or 1 sprig oregano*

Sprout whole-wheat or rye berries, keeping some of the initial soak-water in the fridge until sprouts are ready.

"Salt" the sprouts lightly. Run them through the blender with a little reserved soak-water to blend.

Spoon onto an oiled cookie sheet and dry in the sun or in a food dehydrator, or a very low (not above 110° F.) oven. Break into bite-size pieces. Makes 2 dozen tiny crackers.

On top? How about this quicky "jam"? Chop tomato and puree with basil leaves or oregano. Season with any Salt-free Salt.

Less than 100 calories for a mouthful of cracker and a dab of jam

Carrot Cornbread

Sugar-free.

> 2 cups whole-wheat flour
> 1 cup cornmeal
> 1 tablespoon aluminum-free low-sodium baking powder
> 1 tablespoon allspice or cinnamon plus nutmeg
> ½ cup corn oil
> 1½ cups fresh carrot juice
> ½ cup corn kernels
> ½ cup grated carrots

Preheat oven to 350° F. Mix first 4 dry ingredients in a large bowl.

Mix next 4 wet ingredients in a separate bowl.

Blend wet ingredients with dry ingredients. Pour batter into a well-oiled 8″ × 8″ × 2″ baking pan.

Bake for about ½ hour or until a cake tester comes out clean and the top of the bread turns a little crusty.

Cut into squares and serve warm. Makes 12 squares.

Less than 150 calories per square

Taster's Choice Muffins

> 1½ cups unprocessed miller's bran
> 1 cup whole-wheat flour
> ½ cup raisins
> ¼ cup chopped walnuts or almonds
> 1 teaspoon baking soda
> 6 herb teas, loose or bags
> 1 egg, beaten
> ¼ cup honey
> 2 tablespoons oil
> 1 teaspoon vanilla
> ¾ cup nonfat milk

Preheat oven to 375° F. Blend first 5 ingredients in mixing bowl. Combine remaining ingredients in a separate bowl and stir thoroughly.

Pour over dry ingredients and stir until just blended.

To make 6 different-flavored muffins—2 of each flavor—pour batter ⅔ full into greased muffin pans. Stir ¼ teaspoon herb tea leaves into each cup using 1 flavor for 2 muffins.

Bake 12 minutes. Makes 20 to 24 muffins.

VARIATION: Instead of a frosting, sprinkle muffins with nuts or seeds before baking.

Less than 125 calories per muffin

Salad Bars

A bread substitute.

> 1 carrot
> 1 small zucchini
> 1 small onion
> 4 tablespoons wheat germ
> 2 tablespoons cornmeal
> 3 eggs
> 1 tablespoon minced parsley
> vegetable oil

Preheat oven to 325° F. Grate the carrot, zucchini, and onion together. Mix with the wheat germ and cornmeal.

Separate two of the eggs. Beat the yolks with the whole egg and add to the vegetable mixture. Beat the two remaining egg whites stiff but not dry.

Add the parsley to the vegetable mixture. Gently fold in the egg whites. Bake in a greased pan for 20 minutes. Cool. Carefully cut into "bars." Makes about 18 patties.

VARIATION: These patties may be spiced up with any fresh herbs from your garden.

Less than 125 calories per patty

20 Carrots Bread I

¼ cup molasses
3 cups lukewarm carrot juice or vegetable water
3 tablespoons baking yeast
3 tablespoons vegetable oil
½ cup wheat germ
8 cups whole-wheat flour
2 cups grated carrots

Add the molasses to the carrot juice, stir in the yeast, cover, and let stand 10 minutes or until the yeast is bubbly.

Add the oil to the yeast mixture.

Mix the wheat germ with 5 cups of the flour. Add the flour mixture to the yeast and beat well. Cover with a cloth. Let rise about 40 minutes.

Stir in the carrots, add flour, a cup at a time, until the dough is workable. Knead on a floured board 10 minutes. Place the dough in an oiled bowl, turning to oil the dough. Cover and set to rise for about 45 minutes or until doubled.

Punch the dough down. Turn it out on a floured board and let it rest 10 minutes. Meanwhile, oil three breadpans.

Knead the dough 3 to 4 turns. Form 3 loaves. Place the loaves seam side down in the pans, cover, and set to rise about 45 minutes. During the last 10 minutes of rise, heat the oven to 375° F. Bake 45 minutes.

NOTE: Where can you put your bread dough to rise where it's warm and roomy? Try your wok. Oil the dough, oil the wok, and pop on the lid. To further hasten rising, run hot water over the lid first.

Less than 100 calories per slice

20 Carrots Bread II

2¼ cups unbleached whole-wheat or pastry flour
4 teaspoons baking powder
¼ teaspoon ginger
1½ teaspoons cinnamon
1 cup quick-cooking oats
3 large eggs
⅔ cup or less honey
½ cup oil
¼ cup firmly packed date sugar (optional)
2 cups lightly packed, coarsely shredded pared carrots
⅔ cup chopped almonds

Preheat oven to 325° F. In a large bowl stir together flour, baking powder, ginger, and cinnamon; stir in oats.

In a separate bowl, beat together eggs, honey, oil, and date sugar until blended.

Add flour mixture, stir just until dry ingredients are moistened. Stir in carrots and almonds.

Turn into an oiled 9″ × 5″ × 3″ loaf pan. Bake until a cake tester inserted in center comes out clean (1 hour and 15 minutes).

Cool on wire rack for 10 minutes; loosen edges and turn out on rack; turn right side up. Cool completely. The top will be delightfully flat with only one or two small cracks. Although the crust is on the crisp side, the loaf may be sliced several hours after cooling. The crust will soften after storage in a tightly closed plastic bag.

Less than 150 calories per slice

Blue Chip Breakfast Chips

>   2 cups bran
>   2 cups whole-wheat flour
>   ½ cup nonfat dry milk powder
>   3 tablespoons brewer's yeast
>   1 teaspoon Salt-free Salt I, II, or III (see pp. 60–61)
>   ¼ cup safflower oil
>   1 tablespoon molasses or honey
>   1 cup water

Combine first 5 ingredients. Preheat oven to 350° F.

Make a well in the center and add oil, molasses or honey, and water. Mix well, then roll out between two sheets of waxed paper as thin as possible. (It is easier to divide the dough into 3 or 4 pieces to roll.)

Place rolled dough on oiled cookie sheets and bake 15 to 20 minutes, until lightly browned and crisp. If dough is not completely baked and dry to touch, turn the oven off and let dough remain until it is easily broken into pieces.

Break into small chips by placing in a plastic bag and rolling bag with a rolling pin. Store in an airtight container. Makes 1 pound. One ounce (¼ cup) equals 4.5 grams protein.

Less than 120 calories per ounce

One Potato, Two Potato Puffs

>   2 large potatoes, chopped
>   ½ cup water
>   1 egg
>   1 onion, diced or grated
>   ¼ teaspoon baking powder

Preheat oven to 350° F. Set blender on "grate," and blend potatoes with ½ cup water for a few seconds.

Pour into fine strainer, pressing potatoes with back of spoon to drain off all possible liquid.

Return potatoes to blender, add remaining ingredients, and blend at low speed for a few seconds.

Spoon into greased muffin pan cups, filling each one ⅔ full. Bake 45 minutes. Makes 12 to 16 puffs.

Less than 100 calories per puff

CEREALS

Puffed Wheat

It isn't shot from guns but a bowlful provides plenty of big gun nourishment.

> 2 tablespoons vegetable or nut oil
> 2 handfuls wheat, rye, or triticale
> wheat germ
> bran
> brewer's yeast

In a cast iron skillet with tight fitting cover put vegetable or nut oil, and heat covered. When very hot (not smoking), toss in whole grain.

Stir to coat grains, clap on cover, and agitate over burner until grans "pop." (Puffed grain will not "explode" or triple in size like popcorn.) Eat hot with sprinkle of wheat germ, bran, and a good-tasting brewer's yeast.

Less than 75 calories per handful

Breakfast Sundae I

> 1 cup granola or toasted rolled oats
> ½ cup blueberries
> ½ cup plain yogurt

Mix granola and blueberries and alternate in layers with yogurt in parfait glasses, large brandy snifters, champagne glasses, or banana-split dessert dishes. Makes 2 cups.

Less than 150 calories per cup

Breakfast Sundae II

2 bananas, peeled and sliced
1 cup strawberries
1 cup pineapple cubes
2 oranges, peeled and sectioned
½ cup granola
½ cup plain yogurt

Combine fruit and granola. Pour yogurt over fruit-granola mixture. Serve immediately. Makes 4 cups.

HINT: Keep those empty yogurt containers. They make great seedling starters. Wash, poke drainage holes in the bottom, add soil, and plant seeds. Tear the cup away when you're ready to transplant.

Less than 250 calories per cup

"Shredded" Wheaties

Sprout ½ cup presoaked whole-wheat berries in a tube sprouter (available at many health food stores), or in a can with ends removed.

After 4 to 5 days, when seeds are mature and fully sprouted, remove tube and slice the resulting "loaf" into ¾-inch "biscuit" rounds.

Toast in a low oven until crunchy, dry, and fragrant. Dribble with hot buttered maple syrup or honey, and serve. Or cover with cream and fruit and eat cold.

VARIATION: Sprout ¼ cup wheat kernels with ¼ cup whole rye.

Less than 100 calories per 4-inch biscuit

Museli

3 tablespoons quick-cooking oats
1½ tablespoons whole bran
2 teaspoons sunflower seeds
1–2 tablespoons chopped nuts
2 tablespoons raisins
2 grated carrots
1–2 teaspoons honey
milk

Combine ingredients in individual bowl. Pour cold milk on cereal to cover, and enjoy!

Less than 200 calories per bowlful

Proteena

⅔ quart boiling water, scalded skim milk, or hot fruit juice
millet, cracked wheat, cracked buckwheat, or steel-cut
    oats, et cetera
1 cup nuts

Before going to bed, pour water, skim milk, or fruit juice into a large thermos. Fill two thirds full.

Stir in any whole-grain cereal, almost to top. Close up tightly. It cooks while you sleep.

Uncap next morning, sweeten to taste, add a handful of protein-rich nuts, and dig right in. May also be prepared in a crock pot overnight. Use the lowest setting.

NOTE: If you think nuts are a no-no, consider this: One handful of high-energy almonds gives you 50 percent fewer calories than potato chips, plus iron, calcium, and magnesium.

Less than 100 calories per ½ cup unsweetened grain

DESSERTS

Watermelon Ice

> ½ *small watermelon, peeled, seeded, and cut into 1-inch*
> *chunks (6 cups)*
> 2 *tablespoons honey or apple juice concentrate*
> 1 *tablespoon lemon juice*
> ¼ *teaspoon kelp or ascorbic acid*

Early in day or up to 1 month ahead blend in covered blender at low speed 1 cup watermelon chunks with honey or apple juice concentrate, lemon juice, and kelp or ascorbic acid until smooth. Add remaining watermelon and blend a few seconds longer until smooth. Pour into 9″ × 9″ baking pan. Freeze until partially frozen, about 1½ hours.

Spoon watermelon mixture into large chilled bowl; with mixer at medium speed, beat until fluffy but still frozen. Return mixture to baking pan; cover; freeze until firm, about 1½ hours.

To serve, let ice stand at room temperature about 10 minutes to soften slightly. Then, with spoon, scrape across surface of ice to create a fine "snowlike" texture. Spoon into dessert dishes. Makes 10 servings.

Less than 50 calories per serving

Tofu Whipped Cream

> 1⅓ *cups fresh mashed, well-drained tofu*
> 3 *tablespoons mild honey (more or less to taste)*
> ½ *teaspoon vanilla*
> 2 *tablespoons raw cashew butter*

Combine ingredients in blender. Whip until smooth and creamy. Serve chilled. Makes 1⅔ cups.

Less than 100 calories per tablespoon

Razz Ma Tazz

Calorie-reduced raspberry-peach melba.

> ½ cup fresh or frozen sugar-free raspberries or
>   boysenberries
> 1 teaspoon honey
> dash cinnamon
> 2 ripe peaches
> ¼ cup Ricotta cheese, or ½ cup plain low-fat yogurt

Thaw raspberries or boysenberries, if using frozen fruit. Then press through a sieve to extract juice and pulp. Discard seeds. Blend honey into fruit pulp and add dash of cinnamon. Set aside.

When ready to serve, peel peaches and cut in half. Remove pits and place peaches in four dessert dishes. Beat Ricotta cheese or yogurt with spoon to make light and fluffy and fill centers of peach halves. Spoon melba sauce over all. Makes 4 servings.

Less than 75 calories per serving

Big Red (60-second Sugar-free Apple Sauce)

> 1 large sweet apple (such as Winesap), unpeeled
> 1 cup fresh or frozen strawberries

Chop apple and put in blender with fresh or frozen strawberries and puree. Makes 2 cups.

VARIATION: Substitute raspberries and add 1 to 2 teaspoons rosehip powder for heightened color and nutrition.

Less than 150 calories per cup

Lemon-up Pie

> 1 cup Vegetable Milk (see p. 64)
> 1 cup water
> 1 tablespoon butter
> 7 tablespoons honey, or sweeten to taste
> 4 tablespoons cornstarch or arrowroot
> 1 lemon rind, grated
> ¼ cup lemon juice
> 2 small zucchini or 10 ounces, peeled, sliced, and liquefied
>   in blender
> 2 egg yolks
> 2 egg whites
> 1 8-inch pie shell, baked

Preheat oven to 400° F. Heat Vegetable Milk, water, butter, and 6 tablespoons honey together. While this mixture heats, combine cornstarch, lemon rind, and juice, and add to zucchini.

Cook, stirring constantly, until thick. Beat egg yolks and add a little hot zucchini mixture to them, stirring well.

Then put yolks into the hot zucchini mixture and cook about 1 minute. Remove from heat.

Pour into a baked pie shell (or omit to reduce calories) and top with meringue made by beating egg whites until stiff, then adding 1 tablespoon warmed honey slowly while continuing to beat.

Bake until golden brown (about 5 minutes). Cool and serve. Makes one 12-slice pie.

Less than 100 calories per slice

Tootsie Frootsie (Sugar-free Sherbet)

I:
Blend 2 apples and 2 bananas with a few drops of water. Spoon into sherbet glasses. Garnish with crushed nuts or toasted wheat sprouts.

II:
Refrigerate 2 cups bananas and 2 cups figs soaked overnight. Blend with soak-water until creamy. Chill. Sprinkle with lecithin granules or toasted oats.

III:
Puree 1 very ripe peeled mango with ¼ cup orange juice concentrate. Spoon into cups. Chill until firm.
    VARIATION: Reduce liquid and use any of the above as fruit jams.

Less than 200 calories per cup

Spare Pear

> *1 ripe Comice pear*
> *crushed raw walnuts or almonds*
> *peanut or cashew butter*

Slice pear in half and scoop out seeds.
Sprinkle nuts in both cavities. Top with a thin layer of honey or peanut butter and "glue" back together. A good fridge-raider snack or brown-baggie dessert.

Stuffed Oranges

2 navel oranges, halved
1 pint sugar-free orange or lemon sherbet or frozen yogurt

Scoop out pulp from navel oranges. Save shells. Puree pulp in container of electric blender. Pour into chilled bowl.

Beat in orange or lemon sherbet or frozen yogurt quickly. Freeze in shallow pan, about 1½ hours.

When just firm, mound in orange shells, cover, and keep frozen until ready. Makes 4 servings.

TIP: It's simple to grow your own dwarf orange, lime, lemon, or grapefruit trees from seed. Halve the oranges and scoop out the pulp. Then shellac the outside of the orange skins to prevent rotting. Fill each skin with about 1 inch of your favorite soil and fertilizer. For best results, use liquid seaweed and plant three seeds in each. Put air holes in the sides of the skins and place the skins in a tray. Keep the skin-pots in filtered sunlight and water sparingly. After several weeks the seeds will sprout and after 4 to 6 months the roots will come through the skins. Then stand aside and watch them grow.

Less than 200 calories per serving

Dieter's Pie Crust

2 cups quick-cooking oats
1 cup unsweetened apple sauce

Preheat oven to 350° F. Combine ingredients in a bowl and then press into 2 lightly greased pie pans. Bake 25 minutes. Cool. Fill with cold pudding or fruit puree.

Less than 100 calories per slice

20 Carrots Cake

Sweetened with carrots and fruit.

> *2 eggs*
> *¾ cup vegetable oil*
> *¾ cup powdered milk*
> *1 cup grated carrots*
> *½ cup well-drained crushed pineapple*
> *1 cup whole-wheat pastry flour or unbleached white flour*
> *1½ teaspoons baking powder*
> *¼ teaspoon Salt-free Salt I, II, or III (see pp. 60–61)*
> *2 teaspoons cinnamon*
> *¼ cup honey (optional)*

Preheat oven to 350° F. Combine first 5 ingredients in a bowl and beat.

Then add remaining ingredients and mix well. Spoon into a greased, floured cake or loaf pan.

Bake for 45 minutes. Cut into 12 squares.

Less than 200 calories per square

20 Carrots Sherbet

> *1 quart fresh carrot juice*
> *1 can (6-ounces) frozen orange juice concentrate*
> *3 very ripe medium-size bananas*
> *3 tablespoons honey (optional)*

Place all ingredients in blender. Puree until smooth. Pour mixture into a pan and chill in freezer until almost frozen.

Puree again. Return to pan and cover with plastic wrap. Refreeze. Makes 5 cups.

Less than 200 calories per cup

Potato Candy

¾ cup unseasoned mashed potatoes
⅓ cup or less honey
¾ cup pure peanut butter
1 cup finely chopped sprouts

Mix well the potatoes, honey, and peanut butter.
Stir in sprouts. Chill.
Roll into a log and slice. Or shape into small balls for snacking.

Less than 50 calories per ball

Rock Bottoms

The candy bar alternative.

2 tablespoons honey
1 tablespoon lecithin granules
2 teaspoons toasted wheat germ
2 tablespoons sunflower seeds
4 tablespoons shelled pistachio nuts
1 tablespoon seedless raisins (optional)

Combine honey, lecithin granules, wheat germ, seeds, and nuts. Blend till a ball is formed.
Add raisins; mix well.
Press until flat. Set in the refrigerator until cold. Cut into 2-inch circles or squares.
TIP: Pistachios outrank all other fruits, vegetables, and nuts as a source of potassium and iron. And they contain less fat and fewer calories than all other nuts.

Less than 50 calories per 1-ounce square

Lime Sublime Cheesecake

¾ cup wheat germ or bran
½ cup ground nuts
3 tablespoons safflower oil
pinch of cinnamon
8 ounces low-fat cream cheese, softened
1½ cups drained cottage cheese
3 eggs
2 tablespoons lime or lemon juice
½ teaspoon grated lime rind
¼ cup honey
¼ cup yogurt

Preheat oven to 350° F. Mix first 4 ingredients in a bowl and press into a 9-inch pie pan. Reserve 2 tablespoons of crumb mixture for later use.

Combine remaining ingredients with a mixer, beating until light and fluffy.

Pour into crumb-lined pie pan. Bake for 20 minutes. Remove and sprinkle remaining crumbs on top. Return to oven and bake 5 minutes more. Makes 8 servings.

VARIATION: Make a Lime Sublime pudding by omitting crust. Batter may be poured into 6 greased custard cups and baked at 350° F. for 15 minutes.

NOTE: Soaking your whole citrus fruit in hot water 15 minutes increases the juice yield.

Less than 200 calories per serving

Toad in a Tropical Hole

2 small ripe papayas
vegetable oil
4 small eggs
chopped parsley
2 tablespoons butter

Preheat oven to 375° F. Cut papayas in half. Scoop out seeds.* Hollow out insides slightly to make cavity larger. Brush insides with oil.

Slip an egg in each half. Sprinkle with parsley and dot with butter. Bake 20 to 25 minutes or until eggs are set. Makes 4 servings.

Parsley provides manganese, calcium, potassium, magnesium, and iron. Eggs? They're a first-rate source of sulphur, selenium, and B_{12}.

Less than 300 calories per serving

Carrot Cake Cookies

¾ cup water
1 cup finely grated, squeezed carrots
⅔ cup oil
1 cup honey
1 egg
2 cups pastry flour
2 teaspoons baking powder
1 teaspoon pure vanilla extract
½ teaspoon fresh squeezed lemon juice

* Reserve. Dry at room temperature. Crush. Use as a nonirritating "fruit pepper."

Preheat oven to 400° F. Add the water to the carrot pulp in a small saucepan and cook over a very low heat for 10 minutes, stirring often to keep the pulp from scorching. (One cup of cooked carrots has 16,000 I.U. of vitamin A which is three times the RDA.)

Meanwhile, beat the oil and honey together in a bowl, then beat in the egg. Stir in cooked carrot pulp, flour, and baking powder.

Add vanilla extract and lemon juice. Stir and spoon the dough out onto a greased cookie sheet. Bake 12 to 15 minutes. Makes 24 cookies.

Less than 75 calories per cookie

Calorie-Trimmed Pie Crust

> *1 cup whole-wheat flour*
> *⅔ cup finely ground popped corn * (use blender or electric mill)*
> *¼ cup finely chopped nuts*
> *2 tablespoons date sugar*
> *¼ cup butter or margarine*

Preheat oven to 350° F. Combine all ingredients except butter or margarine and mix well.

Add butter and mash with a pastry blender or two knives until a coarse meal is formed.

Press into a buttered 9-inch pan. Bake 15 minutes. Cool and fill. Makes enough for 8–10 slices.

HINT: Dip pie pan in warm water for 2 minutes before inserting your crust and it won't crumble or stick after baking.

Less than 100 calories per slice

* Less than 60 calories in an unbuttered cupful.

Water Chestnut Jelly *(Gelatin)*

> *3-4 pieces fresh or canned water chestnuts*
> *8 tablespoons water chestnut flour*
> *3 tablespoons honey*
> *1⅔ cups water*
> *2 envelopes unflavored gelatin*
> *plain low-fat yogurt*

Slice the water chestnuts into thin matchsticks. Blend the water chestnut flour with honey and water in a saucepan. Bring to a boil and simmer over low heat. Add the gelatin and stir for 1 minute.

Pour the mixture into a well-greased, deep-sided, flat-bottomed dish. Sprinkle the water chestnut strips evenly over the mixture, and allow them to sink into the liquid. When cool, place the dish in the refrigerator for 2 to 3 hours, by which time the liquid should have set.

Turn the jelly onto a flat dish and cut into 6 even pieces. Serve each piece with a dollop of low-fat yogurt. The contrast between the texture of the shredded water chestnut and the water chestnut jelly is memorable. Makes 6 servings.

Less than 60 calories per square

20 Carrots Cheesecake

High in nutrients.

> *2 cups cooked carrots*
> *2 cups cottage cheese*
> *4 eggs*
> *⅓ cup or less honey*
> *¼ teaspoon nutmeg*
> *1 teaspoon cinnamon*
> *½ teaspoon ginger*
> *¼ teaspoon cloves*

Preheat oven to 325° F. Put all ingredients in the blender and whip until smooth.

Pour mixture into a 1-quart baking dish. Set the dish in a pan of hot water and bake for about 50 minutes or until a knife inserted in the center comes out clean. Serve chilled. Makes 8 servings.

Less than 150 calories per serving

Sugar-free Icings

And the last shall be best. When is a muffin a cupcake? When you frost it. Here are three no-sucrose ways to have your cake and eat it, too. Makes enough for one layer or six cupcakes.

YOGURT ICING:
>   *½ cup plain yogurt*
>   *¼ cup raw honey or maple syrup*
>   *⅓ cup noninstant milk powder*
>   *1 tablespoon lime or lemon juice*
>   *1 tablespoon soft butter*

Beat all ingredients in bowl until mixture is smooth. To thicken add more milk powder. Icing solidifies as it sets.

MOCK BUTTERSCOTCH FROSTING:
>   *12 pitted dates*
>   *apple juice*
>   *1 tablespoon wheat germ*

Puree dates with a bit of apple juice until thick and smooth. Stir in wheat germ. Spread it on.

MAKE-BELIEVE ICING:
Place a paper doily over cake or cupcakes and sift on powdered milk or arrowroot spiked with a bit of cinnamon, mace, ginger, or nutmeg.

VIII
Vegetable Remedies

When your nose, your stomach, your head refuse to suffer in congested silence, do you jump? Don't. The pills we swallow are often bitter pills. Nature sometimes has a better way. . . .

Fighting a fiber deficiency?

Ruffage *(Lettuce-free High Fiber Salad)*

> *1 medium-size bunch parsley*
> *1 small clove garlic*
> *2 tablespoons olive oil*
> *½ lemon*

Cut the stems off the bunch of parsley and chop the leaves coarsely. Divide on 2 small salad plates. Chop the garlic clove very fine and sprinkle over each plate.

Drip 1 tablespoon of olive oil and the juice of ¼ lemon over each; stir lightly.

155

VARIATION: Try a pinch of dill weed or raw onion rings that have been marinated a few hours in vinegar.

A half cup (4 ounces) of fresh chopped parsley has approximately 10,000 units of vitamin A; almost 200 milligrams of vitamin C (more than a similar amount of oranges); generous amounts of calcium, iron, phosphorus, and potassium; and traces of iodine, copper, and manganese. Parsley in any form—fresh, as tea, or as juice—is an excellent diuretic and as such is used in the treatment of physical problems where edema is a factor. Because they are often related, inflammation of the kidneys and urinary tract respond well to parsley. As a natural source of iron, it has been used to treat anemia and menstrual problems.

Another curly green cure? A mouthful of parsley also makes a good breath freshener.

Fighting fatigue? Here's a liquid asset.

B-8 Juice

> 2 cups vegetable cocktail juice or Broth (see p. 82)
> 1-3 teaspoons brewer's yeast (shop around, some taste
>   better than others)

Process in blender until smooth.

VARIATIONS: Add kelp, vitamin C powder, dry vegetable flakes.

Fighting a cold?

Vitamin C Soup

> 1 cup seedless rosehips *
> 1 quart water
> 2 tablespoons honey (or more if you like it sweeter)

* One of the richest known natural sources of vitamin C next to acerola berries.

8 cassia buds (optional)
½ teaspoon ground cinnamon
yogurt or sour cream (optional)

Soak rosehips in water overnight.

The next day, put them into a saucepan along with the water, honey, cassia buds, and cinnamon. Simmer for about ½ hour.

Remove from heat, cool slightly, strain, whirl in blender until smooth; chill and serve with sour cream or yogurt. Serves 4.

HINT: To thicken a soup after it's left the soup pot, grate in 3 tablespoons raw potato per bowl. This also blots up any excess oils.

Feel a sneeze coming on? Scoop a remedy.

Ascorbic Acid Ice Milk

8 ounces pitted dates
½ cup boiling water
1 cup cold water
1 cup milk or yogurt
1 teaspoon grated lemon rind
4 teaspoons lemon juice
1–2 teaspoons powdered vitamin C or rosehip powder
    (available from any pharmacy or health food store)

Blend dates and boiling water in blender until pureed. Stir in cold water, milk or yogurt, lemon rind, juice, and vitamin C powder.

Freeze until almost firm. Then beat until smooth.

Turn into 9″ × 9″ × 2″ pan. Place wrap on top. Freeze until firm. Makes 6 servings.

VARIATION: Figs or apricots may be used instead of dates.

Upset stomach?

Alka-Settlers

Nature's own Tums.

CITRUS SPRINKLES:
Dry the rind from a large grapefruit (the oil and bioflavonoids are remedial). Dry in a warm kitchen overnight. Grind in blender until gritty. Use ½ teaspoon for relief. Suck on it, then chew slowly.

BAKING SODA "SODA":
Combine lemon juice, ½ to 1 teaspoon bicarbonate of soda, and sparkling mineral water. Sip. Baking soda is basically an antacid *without* aspirin, caffeine, or those other assorted additives—an effective and fast neutralizer.

OPTIONAL: For a high-C soda, add ¼ teaspoon powdered vitamin C.

ALOE LOVIN' SPOONFUL:
One tablespoon of aloe vera gel or liquid or powder taken in 2 cups of fruit juice 30 minutes before meals, or raw cabbage juice mixed with a little carrot juice, provides relief plus.

What else? Dill seeds, fennel seeds, ginger root, peppermint, and last but not least, warm milk. Not only simplicity itself, it may indeed be the safest solution of all.

Headache?

Almond Aspirins

> *1 cup honey*
> *¾ cup whole raw almonds, pecans, or Brazil nuts*
> *½–1 cup unsweetened coconut as needed*

Heat the honey, stirring to the firm ball stage (240° F.). Remove from heat.

Quickly, using tongs or sugar-cube pincers, dip each nut into the hot honey, then into the coconut. Set the "bearded nuts" aside on wax paper until dry.

A nut is something to take to heart when you have a headache. If you chew four or five almonds, you'll have enough of a natural pain-killing substance called salicylate to equal one aspirin, say researchers Dr. Ivan Danhof, professor of physiology at the University of Texas Medical School at Dallas, and Dr. Michael Rosenbaum, specialist in nutrition at the federally funded Commonweal Clinic in Bolinas, California. In fact, ten to twelve almonds may put enough salicylate into your bloodstream to provide relief without distressing the stomach lining, plus protein, potassium, and moderate amounts of the natural fats that help keep you thin. Other foods rich in salicylate are potatoes, apricots, and fruits.

Constipated?

Ex-Flax

High-fiber all-vegetable laxative.

> *1 cup pitted prunes*
> *1 cup raisins*
> *1 cup finely grated carrot*
> *3 teaspoons flax seeds*
> *powdered carob or milk*
> *cinnamon*

Put ingredients through food grinder (pour a little boiling water through, too, to prevent sticking). Form mixture into tiny balls. Roll in powdered carob or milk spiked with cinnamon. Chill. Take 3 or 4 a day, as needed.

Treating hoarseness, or a sandpaper throat?

Nature's Penicillin

> *24 garlic cloves*
> *raw honey*

Peel garlic cloves and put them in a jar. Add raw honey, a little at a time over a couple of days, until the jar is full.

Set in a sunlit window until the garlic has turned somewhat opaque and all the garlic flavor has been transferred to the honey.

USES: Garlic is a honey of a way to meet a cold head on. Known as "nature's penicillin," the Greeks and Romans ate it as a health protector, aphrodisiac, antiseptic, and expectorant. This "recipe" makes an excellent cough syrup or a liquid cough drop Take a teaspoon every few hours or whenever necessary. Remember this is a concentrate: *One teaspoonful represents many cloves of garlic.* For a child, dilute each spoonful with water. Garlic honey also soothes a sore throat. As an external application for acne or herpes it is both healing, soothing, and slightly anesthetic. It can be used as a glaze on baked vegetables, too.

VARIATION: For extra healing power, stir in ¼ teaspoon ascorbic acid per 8-oz. cup.

Sore throat? Try these.

Carrot Contac

Cold gotcha? Let a carrot save you. Squeeze fresh carrot juice or open a can. It's rich in calcium, zinc, and infection-fighting vitamin A. Pour over maple sugar lumps.

Ginger Lozenge

Peel and thinly slice a fresh ginger root. Suck throughout the day for hoarseness. Double your pleasure. You get better chances by alternating with hot ginger tea.

Stuffed head?

Sergeant Pepper Sinus Cure

Capsicum comes from the Greek, *Kapto,* meaning "I bite," which red peppers do and green peppers don't. But bell peppers are all good for what ails you if what ails you is sinus trouble. Try this (also a good A.M. rouser):

> *1 cup fresh orange juice*
> *¼ teaspoon cayenne (the fresher the better)*
> *½ raw green pepper, chopped (optional)*

Put in blender jar and puree.

IX

Charts for the Vegetarian Weight Loss Dieter

FIBER FINDER

Remember, fiber can't be used or stored as fat.

Foods with No Fiber:

> Meat
> Fish
> Poultry
> Sugar and sweet syrups
> Eggs
> Dairy products
> Fats and oils
> Candy

Foods Which Have Lost Fiber in Processing:

Refined cereal products (macaroni, white rice, white bread)
Dehydrated potatoes
French fried potatoes
Potato chips and other fried snacks *
Fruit juices
Canned fruit
Canned vegetables

Foods with Good to Excellent Fiber Content:

Wheat bran
Wheat germ
Whole-grain cereal products
Nuts and seeds, nut butters *
Legumes
Sprouts
Fresh vegetables—particularly raw †
Frozen vegetables ‡
Frozen fruit
Dried fruit *

* Substantial fiber but also high in calories, thus making it an inefficient source of fiber.

† Vegetables are the dieter's best source. Super "F" vegetables include artichokes, as-paragus, green beans, broccoli, brussels sprouts, cauliflower, celery, cucumbers, and dan-delion greens (knew they were good for something!). Also eggplant, kale, lettuce, green pepper, radishes, and turnip tops are good. For example: one cup of green beans contains only 52 calories and 2 grams of fiber. Sixteen Brazil nuts also contain 2 grams of fiber and 646 calories.

‡ Fiber is lost in processing.

TOTALS: VEGETABLES FOR DAILY VITAMINS

Vitamin	Recommended Daily Allowance	Vegetable	Milligrams per 3½-ounce serving
Calcium	Adult—800 mg.	raw beet greens	119
		raw broccoli	103
		cooked broccoli	88
		raw collard greens	203
		raw kale	179
		cooked kale	134
		raw parsley	203
		raw turnip greens	246
		cooked turnip greens	184
Iron	Adult—10 mg.	cooked lima beans	2.5
		raw Swiss chard	3.2
		cooked Swiss chard	1.8
		raw kale	2.2
		raw New Zealand spinach	2.6
		cooked New Zealand spinach	1.5
		raw immature peas in pods	1.9
		cooked immature peas in pods	1.8
		dry pumpkin or squash seed kernels	11.2
		raw spinach	3.1
		cooked spinach	2.2
Potassium	Adult—1,875 to 5,625 mg.	cooked lima beans	422
		raw Swiss chard	550
		cooked Swiss chard	321
		raw garden cress	606
		cooked garden cress	353
		raw New Zealand spinach	795
		cooked New Zealand spinach	463
		potatoes baked in their skins	503
		potatoes boiled in their skins	407
		potatoes mashed with milk	261
		raw spinach	470
		baked butternut squash	609

Vitamin	Recommended Daily Allowance	Vegetable	Milligrams per 3½-ounce serving
Vitamin A	Adult—1,000 mg.	raw carrots	11,000
		cooked carrots	10,500
		raw Swiss chard	6,500
		cooked Swiss chard	5,400
		raw garden cress	9,300
		cooked garden cress	7,700
		raw dandelion greens	14,000
		raw kale	8,900
		raw parsley	8,500
		baked butternut squash	6,400
		raw spinach	8,100
Phosphorus	Adult—800 mg.	cooked lima beans	121
		cooked corn	89
		cooked peas	99
		dry pumpkin or squash seed kernels	1,144
		baked butternut squash	72
Thiamine	Adult—1.4 mg.	raw asparagus	.18
		cooked asparagus	.16
		cooked lima beans	.18
		raw peas	.28
		cooked peas	.22
		pumpkin and squash seeds	.24
		raw collard greens	.20
		raw turnip greens	.21
Riboflavin	Adult—1.6 mg.	raw asparagus	.20
		cooked asparagus	.18
		raw beet greens	.22
		cooked beet greens	.15
		raw or cooked collard greens	.31
		raw garden cress	.26
		cooked garden cress	.16
		raw spinach	.20
		cooked spinach	.14
		raw turnip greens	.39
		cooked turnip greens	.24
Niacin	Adult—18 mg.	cooked asparagus spears	1.4
		cooked lima beans	1.3
		cooked collard greens	1.2
		cooked corn on the cob	1.4
		potatoes baked in their skins	1.7
		potatoes boiled in their skins	1.5
		potatoes mashed with milk	1.0
		summer squash and zucchini	1.0

Vitamin	Recommended Daily Allowance	Vegetable	Milligrams per 3½-ounce serving
Vitamin C	Adult—60 mg.	raw broccoli	113
		cooked broccoli	90
		raw cauliflower	78
		cooked cauliflower	55
		raw collard greens	92
		cooked collard greens	46
		raw kale	125
		cooked kale	62
		raw green peppers	128
		cooked green peppers	96

THE LOW CALS

20 BELOW: 20 FOODS WITH APPROXIMATELY 100 CALORIES

1 banana
2 cups plain popcorn
20 stalks celery
1 ounce natural blue cheese
1 slice French bread
80 radishes
1 cup unsweetened apple sauce
1 Bartlett pear
⅕ of a honeydew melon
4 ounces table wine
1 cup plain yogurt
½ cup millet
½ cup cottage cheese
60 average green seedless grapes
4–5 young carrots (3 inches to 4 inches)
1¼ cups skim milk
¾ cup orange juice
2 cups tomato juice
1 medium-size banana
1½ cups strawberries

20 BELOW: 20 FOODS WITH APPROXIMATELY 50 CALORIES

3 ounces tofu
1 small apple
4 tablespoons cottage cheese
1 tangerine
½ cup blackberries
½ fresh grapefruit
½ fresh mango
1 nectarine
⅔ cup cooked collard greens
½ cup unsweetened orange juice
⅓ medium papaya
4 small boiled eggs
⅔ cup soy sprouts
1 cup cooked green beans
¾ cup raw broccoli
1 cup steamed asparagus
1 large baked onion
1 cup plain popcorn
¾ cup sprouted lentils, other legumes

NOTHING DOWN: THE FREE FOODS—
NO CALORIES

Practically calorie-free but satisfying.

Beet greens
Broccoli
Brussels sprouts
Cabbage, Chinese, green, and red
Cauliflower
Celery
Chard
Cucumbers and pickles
Green and red peppers
Leeks
Lettuce, all kinds of greens
Mushrooms
Onions
Parsley
Radishes
Spinach
Sprouts, all kinds
String beans
Unflavored gelatin
Watercress

INDEX

171